Ambitious

INSTRUCTION

Teaching With **Rigor** in the
Secondary Classroom

Brad Cawn

Solution Tree | Press

a division of
Solution Tree

555 North Morton Street
Bloomington, IN 47404
800.733.6786 (toll free) / 812.336.7700
FAX: 812.336.7790

email: info@SolutionTree.com
SolutionTree.com

Visit **go.SolutionTree.com/instruction** to download the free reproducibles in this book.

Printed in the United States of America

Library of Congress Cataloging-in-Publication Data

Names: Cawn, Brad, author.
Title: Ambitious instruction : teaching with rigor in the secondary
    classroom / Brad Cawn.
Description: Bloomington, IN : Solution Tree Press, [2020] | Includes
    bibliographical references and index.
Identifiers: LCCN 2019036848 (print) | LCCN 2019036849 (ebook) | ISBN
    9781947604254 (paperback) | ISBN 9781947604261 (ebook)
Subjects: LCSH: High school teaching. | Active learning. | Classroom
    environment. | School improvement programs.
Classification: LCC LB1737 .C39 2020 (print) | LCC LB1737 (ebook) | DDC
    373.1102--dc23
LC record available at https://lccn.loc.gov/2019036848
LC ebook record available at https://lccn.loc.gov/2019036849

Solution Tree

Jeffrey C. Jones, CEO
Edmund M. Ackerman, President

Solution Tree Press

President and Publisher: Douglas M. Rife
Associate Publisher: Sarah Payne-Mills
Art Director: Rian Anderson
Managing Production Editor: Kendra Slayton
Production Editor: Miranda Addonizio
Content Development Specialist: Amy Rubenstein
Copy Editor: Kate St. Ives
Editorial Assistant and Proofreader: Sarah Ludwig

To my mother:
the most ambitious instructor I know.

ACKNOWLEDGMENTS

This book is truly the sum of its parts and reflects learning, sweat, and tears derived from professional development sessions I've facilitated, college courses I've taught, and feedback I've received from a broad range of educators, administrators, academics, parents, and students. To every student or teacher I taught, to every educator who engaged me at a conference or school, to every person who debated or argued with me—you are the reason this book exists. Thank you.

Big shout-outs to the Solution Tree publishing and professional development staff for their endless patience and support: Alex Ostrom, Amy Rubenstein, Douglas Rife, Kendra Slayton, Macy Hughes, Miranda Addonizio, and Sarah Payne-Mills. I was a year late submitting the manuscript and incredibly antsy in the year it took to get to market—and yet you still emailed me back every time! Wonders never cease.

I'd be remiss if I didn't acknowledge those who provided feedback and encouragement during the long development and gestation period. Sarah Alexander. Shay Bahramirad. Danny White. Why drive yourself crazy when you can drive someone else nuts instead?

And to you, the reader. If you got this far, and are still reading: bless you.

Solution Tree Press would like to thank the following reviewers:

Carrie Chapman
Professor
Minnesota State University
Mankato, Minnesota

Chris George
Assistant Principal
Christiana Middle School
Christiana, Tennessee

Elaine Keeley
Director of Curriculum, Instruction,
  and Staff Development
Merced City School District
Merced, California

TABLE OF CONTENTS

CHAPTER 3
Implementing Ambitious Instruction

CHAPTER 4
Facilitating Ambitious Instruction

CHAPTER 5
Supporting and Sustaining Ambitious Instruction

References and Resources

Index

ABOUT THE AUTHOR

Brad Cawn is a teacher, author, researcher, and trainer who specializes in helping schools and teachers integrate ambitious teaching and learning—inquiry-based instruction, disciplinary literacy, project-based learning, and so on—across the content areas. At the core of this support is an emphasis on the *work* of teaching: professional development that focuses on the design, enactment, and study of instructional practice.

Brad is the author of *Texts, Tasks, and Talk* and was the lead researcher and writer on *Ambitious Leadership*, a Gates Foundation–funded research project on the policies and practices that define 21st century instructional leadership. He has supported and advised some of the United States' largest school districts—including Los Angeles Unified School District, Clark County School District (Las Vegas), and Chicago Public Schools—as well as the U.S. Department of Education and Teach for America. He serves on the faculty of the Association for Supervision and Curriculum Development.

Brad is a former high school English teacher and central office administrator, having directed Chicago Public Schools' rollout of professional learning communities and Common Core training. When not working with schools and districts, he teaches graduate-level coursework on instruction at DePaul University and an undergraduate course on design thinking at Northwestern University, both in the Chicago area.

Brad holds graduate degrees in education and education leadership from Northwestern University and the University of Michigan, respectively; he also holds a master of business administration degree from DePaul University.

To book Brad Cawn for professional development, contact pd@SolutionTree.com.

INTRODUCTION

Redefining Rigor

The task seemed simple enough. "Share your annotations and compare your findings with a partner," the eighth-grade English language arts (ELA) teacher instructed her students, who had read and marked up the claims and reasoning of a nonfiction essay (as articulated in Common Core State Standard RI.8.8; National Governors Association Center for Best Practices [NGA] & Council of Chief State School Officers [CCSSO], 2010) for homework the previous evening. But bigger plans were afoot. After a few minutes of partner work, she merged pairs into table groups of four, charging each group with gathering textual evidence in support of an answer to the overarching problem this lesson and the next would solve, *What does it mean to be free?* She asked groups that finished the task early to consider alternative perspectives and supporting evidence. The teacher circulated around the room, checking for understanding and reminding groups of the class norms—everyone participates, claims must be grounded in evidence from the texts, and so on. When ready, she reconvened the whole class and initiated a discussion in which she asked students to respond to one another's ideas by debating over their responses to the task and utilizing the text to support the strengths and flaws of their peers' arguments. The lesson wrapped up with an exit ticket that prompted students to synthesize their findings on the homework text with previous texts in the unit to develop an initial claim in response to the problem.

Across the hall, the teacher's colleague assigned the same homework to her students. Here, the teacher reread a portion of the text aloud, pausing to let students share their annotations; she shared her annotations when students did not share their own. She facilitated a whole-class discussion based on students' opinion of the text, acknowledging each student's comments before calling on another to participate. When she finished the questioning, she guided the whole class back toward the main idea of the unit she had shared a couple of times previously. She gave exit slips that asked students to summarize the main points of the different opinions they had heard.

Two classrooms. Same grade. Same hallway. Same skills. Same text.

And yet.

We register the differences between these two examples as obvious, palpable. The second example feels familiar: we've seen it or done it ourselves; it's fine. But the first feels like something else: comprehensive, challenging, complete. We recognize the sensible scaffolding, the rich interactions with texts and problem solving; we appreciate the rich student-to-student talk and argument-focused comprehension building. It's what we aspire to, what we want every classroom, every day, to look like. Anyone would call this rigorous: we know it when we see it.

That's what I aim to do for secondary teachers: make rigor visible. Make it accessible. Make it actionable. And I want to do this for teachers not just within classrooms but across them, so that all students have opportunities to engage in meaningful intellectual work. That's ambitious instruction.

But accomplishing all this requires both authors like myself and school leaders and teachers like yourself to face a hard truth: this idea of *rigor* that has permeated so much talk in education has remained stubbornly elusive in many secondary classrooms. Studies show that a strong majority of classroom tasks do not meet the level of rigor established in the Common Core or state standards (Education Trust, 2015), are formulaic and not engaging (Applebee & Langer, 2012), provide limited opportunities to engage texts meaningfully (Greenleaf & Valencia, 2017; Litman et al., 2017), and rarely encourage the kinds of complex thinking necessary to demonstrate college and career readiness (Marzano & Toth, 2014). More than five hundred hours of instructional time are wasted *per student*, per year, on formulaic tasks that don't encourage complex thinking (TNTP, 2018). Survey after survey of U.S. teachers (Bill and Melinda Gates Foundation, 2014; Kaufman et al., 2016) confirm it: teachers struggle with rigor, and they want and need help to close the gap between their intentions and their actions.

A Clear Definition of Rigor

Closing that gap starts with getting clear on what rigor is and what it means. It isn't the buzzwords—*creativity, 21st century learning, critical thinking*—it's all too easy to nod in agreement when watching a YouTube video on these subjects and then subsequently ignore it. I mean an operational definition, where rigor is a level or kind of work we can feel, see, and do. As anyone who has tried to teach the skill of analysis or evaluation knows, it's a serious challenge to take things we know and do tacitly and adjust them for school-age learners.

Let's start simple, then. At its most elemental, *rigor* is teaching and learning that are *up to standard*—that is, they meet the level of cognitive complexity or challenge of the standards or benchmarks guiding the learning. Note the part about teaching *and* learning: rigor refers to both the instruction—the content or texts provided, the work or assessments administered, and so forth—and the efforts of the students, their understanding, and work. This is the science of rigor. What we ask of students and the instruction we provide for them to achieve it must be in line with our benchmarked expectations for teaching and learning. That's not to say that rigor is inherently, say, the Common Core, or that the Common Core is inherently rigorous—we've all been in enough classrooms that use a textbook purportedly aligned to the standards, or seen a lesson plan with some Common Core State Standards (CCSS) slapped on, to know better. But the foundation for everything is our shared understanding of what students know and are able to do by the end of a given grade, as well as by how we ask students to demonstrate this understanding (for example, college readiness exams like the Partnership for Assessment of Readiness for College and Careers [PARCC] or the Smarter Balanced Assessment Consortium [SBAC], ACT or SAT, and so on). This is *academic* rigor.

Still, this doesn't quite cover the opportunity and challenge that attention to rigor presents. Standards like your state benchmarks or the Common Core, after all, only tell you *what* to teach, and even then, often only focus on general academic or cognitive skills, not content. Leveraging the standards, making them meaningful, requires careful attention to the content and facilitation of these skills—that is, a rigor of method. This is the art of it: we provide the additional teaching and learning supports that go *beyond* the standard. Project-based learning. Socratic seminars. Document-based questions. Investigations. It's the way we facilitate that engenders that 21st century learning, that critical thinking, that creativity. This is *instructional* rigor.

Now, I know what you're thinking: great, more education jargon. But the shift in thinking about rigor is quite simple, as shown in figure I.1 (page 4). Prior to the rollout of new college and career readiness benchmarks like the Common Core, the generally accepted notion of rigor was that it was something produced as a result of students being engaged in their learning. In other words, did students have a choice in how they responded to a task—say, of how to perform or create a product in response to it? Their creativity and interest and talent would be engaged in such a way that they would produce higher-quality work, hence rigor. The new vision, while not necessarily dismissing this notion, foregrounds rigor as the work students must do at *all* times—that is, there is a clear and expected standard for what students should

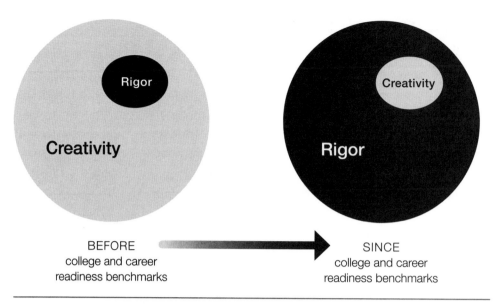

Figure I.1: Rethinking rigor.

know and do, and the emphasis needs to be on ensuring tasks, texts, facilitation, and so forth meet that standard. We can enable creativity through that matching of expectations.

I know this seems simple, almost reductively so. But humor me for a minute.

If you accept the basic premise of the preceding definition of rigor, consider for a minute how so many schools—including, perhaps, your own—are going about addressing it: by examining and applying taxonomies like Benjamin S. Bloom's (1956) or Norman L. Webb's (1997) Depth of Knowledge (DOK). You know what I mean: checking tasks or activities to see under what level of complexity they fall, then trying to up the rigor by changing a verb or making it more open ended. We all do it. It feels straightforward and easy (enough). And, on the surface, it feels right; if there is a common expectation that students should engage in higher-order thinking, shouldn't all instruction be at DOK level 3 (strategic thinking) or 4 (extended thinking)—or the Evaluation level of Bloom's—all the time?

Truly shifting rigor, though, demands more.

If the standards determine what rigor is, we cannot engage in any exercise of assessing or adjusting task rigor without the benchmarks of the standards. Furthermore, because nearly every single content literacy standard in your school's or state's learning objectives involves engagement of texts—class readings and students' own texts—we also cannot reconsider rigor without our texts. And because rigor isn't just the complexity of the task but also the quality of the student work on said task, we certainly cannot reconsider rigor without what students actually do—or, at least, our intended goals, outcomes, and criteria for said work.

So. Tasks matter. Goals matter. What students read matters. This we all know. But lost in our conversations about understanding rigor levels, considering text complexity, and requiring lesson objectives on the board is that these things are not discrete; in fact, their *interaction* in support of student learning determines whether both teacher *and* students can meet that rigor. We can't look at rigor and text complexity as separate issues; they are, in fact, the same (Valencia, Wixson, & Pearson, 2014). We can't look at what we ask students to do as separate from our purpose, nor can we disconnect that purpose from our standardized expectation of what students should be doing; it is not rigor otherwise. After all, complex texts or tasks are the means, not the outcome; the goal is complex, sophisticated student thinking—*that* is rigor.

In short, rigor is in practice, not just planning. It is not determined solely by the language in the task prompt; rather, it is realized in action, through the interaction of reader, content, and activity. Our attention must be on the interaction—including the teacher and student interaction *during* learning—if we are to truly support increased rigor schoolwide. Knowing this, and knowing when we can see it in classrooms or not, distinguishes instructional leaders who make ambitious instruction happen from those who don't (Huff, Preston, Goldring, & Guthrie, 2018).

Thus, when we're in classrooms, when we are reviewing curriculum, when we are thinking about how to help teachers improve their teaching, rigor is both academic and instructional. In plans, it is rich content and tasks that are equal to or above what is expected of students at the given grade level or course; in action, it is enactment that sustains and supports complexity while honoring and encouraging student thinking to support proficiency and mastery in the content and skill. Rigor is a fully realized articulation of good teaching and learning, essentially—the *what* and *how*.

And ambitious instruction is the name for it.

How to Name and Know Ambitious Instruction

Teachers of ambitious instruction are uniquely interested in the *performance* of their students on cognitively complex tasks—that is, their primary focus when planning and delivering instruction is on students' ideas, how they come to know and develop them, and the supports (such as time, modeling, or differentiation) necessary to facilitate them. This is precisely the opposite of so-called "cute" instruction. No Pinterest. No Teachers Pay Teachers. No planning "cool" activities.

But how do you recognize ambitious instruction, anyway? In simplest terms, everything pedagogical is in the service of supporting the intellectual work of your students. That means, among other things, the following (Cobb, Jackson, Henrick, Smith, & the MIST Team, 2018; Lampert & Graziani, 2009; McDonald, Kazemi, & Kavanagh, 2013; Windschitl, Thompson, & Braaten, 2011).

- Tasks focus on key disciplinary ideas, problems, and processes of a given subject area.
- Tasks prioritize reasoning, argumentation, synthesis, and reflection as the essential processes and products of academic work.
- Teachers engage *all* students through structured opportunities to address the demands of these kinds of tasks.
- Teachers are responsive to individual students' learning *during* learning.

In this sense, ambitious instruction is defined both by its attention to the design of certain kinds of instructional activities—that is, ones that best elicit students' understanding and application of rich content—and by a kind of delivery of these activities that is tailored to and interactive with students in moment-to-moment engagement with the work (Lampert & Graziani, 2009; Lee, 2007). This means rigorous tasks that deeply engage students. This means strong instructional support, including structured use of inquiry and feedback, deliberately designed to sustain both students' persistence and resilience when faced with complexity, while also maintaining high expectations for all learners. You can imagine the rest: consistent and deep interactions with texts, meaningful collaboration with and among peers, leveraging both to synthesize and construct arguments, and so on.

This kind of instruction, alas, is exceedingly rare in grades 6–12 classrooms (Goldman, Snow, & Vaughn, 2016; Greenleaf & Valencia, 2017). The results when we do apply it, though? A powerful rebuttal to those who doubt students' ability to do high-level work: research has repeatedly shown that students, especially those with persistent learning challenges, learn more and achieve greater outcomes when what we ask them to do is consistently rigorous and grade-level appropriate (Abedi & Herman, 2010; Boston & Wilhelm, 2017; TNTP, 2018). In short, rigorous instruction can be done. It must be done.

Ambitious Instruction: The Blueprint

And it will. But naming it and doing it, as you know, are not the same when it comes to complex instruction. That's why this is a book of next steps: not just a bunch of tantalizing, frustratingly abstract nouns (*ambitious instruction, rigor*) but a step-by-step breakdown of the will and work necessary to make them come alive in the classroom—a blueprint. To build the foundation, we need to dig deeper and get inside the actual practice involved in teaching ambitiously.

The good news: there's actually nothing here you don't already know. And everything you are going to do for planning and enacting ambitious instruction can be boiled down to a simple mantra: *assign students to solve, in and through multiple modalities, a relevant but grade-appropriate problem of the discipline or content area; structure and sequence your instruction to help them solve it.*

You know this already. Really.

But a little more detail can't hurt. Let me introduce you to the two central tenets of ambitious instruction.

1. **Problem-based learning:** The best pedagogy to help students realize this kind of critical thinking is inquiry based, with clear structures and supports provided by the teacher in order to ensure students' ideas are valued, enabled, and extended. In the pages that follow, you'll find a vision of inquiry built around intellectual problems, collaborative meaning making and discussion, and argumentation—disciplinary literacy with a disciplined focus.

2. **Synthesis:** The kind of learning students should primarily be doing is critical-analytical in nature—that is, individual learners and the class engage in examined, systematic understanding of the arguments and perspectives of both texts and peers. Such a curricular focus, which I will refer to as *intellectual work* throughout the book, centers on interrogating and evaluating relevant problems of a given subject area, positioning students as meaning makers and subject matter as complex and worthy of meaningful exploration.

So far so good, right? The four main components of such instruction, which we'll unpack in subsequent chapters, follow suit.

1. A *high-quality problem* that develops students' content knowledge and discipline-specific problem-solving skills (surprise, surprise).

2. A *performance assessment* designed to answer this problem through synthesis.

3. A *text set*, which is a group of thematically linked texts that functions as the content-area learning in support of the problem.

4. A *module*, which is the road map that guides learners from the launch to the completion of the end assessment—the sequence of content and instruction designed to support preparation for answering the problem.

Figure I.2 (page 8) provides a visual representation of these four segments.

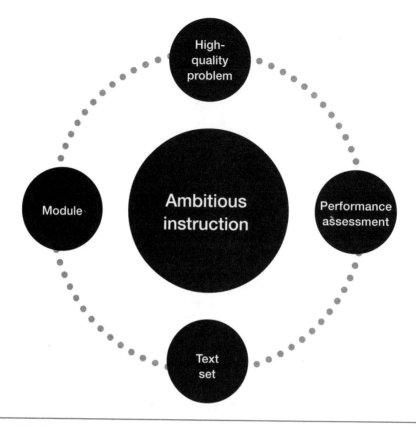

Figure I.2: Core curricular products of ambitious instruction.

Underlying what I've laid out so far, but as yet unstated, is your most precious commodity: time. This kind of teaching and learning is problem driven, exploratory, and requires multiple tasks and activities; it takes time. And it's more than just a matter of the amount of time. We also must think about how we use the available time in service of intellectual learning. Class can't just be lessons as usual. Realizing rigor, in other words, is more than simply asking students to do hard(er) things; it's *designing* instructional time to help them do so.

This means we cannot default to ingrained, preconceived ideas about planning. We have to let go of the notion that the school year comprises a series of units of certain and confined length (for example, four to six weeks), or that each day of instruction is a discrete lesson, to be completed by the end of the instructional time provided that day (that is, the period). There is no evidence that these structures aid either planning or student learning (Willingham, 2018). Instead, think of ambitious instruction as more than just a matter of defining essential understandings and assessments but also a matter of essential use of time—that is, how instruction is to be organized in order to enable students to solve meaningful problems in meaningful ways. Ambitious instruction is also ambitious use of instructional time.

Thinking about the relation between time and ambitious instruction means thinking about instructional rigor in multiple ways.

- **Practice and learning need to be *deep*:** Understanding is tied to the examples and applications students work with, hence students need rich ones.

- **Practice and learning need to be *diverse*:** Students will need several chances for their understanding to move from superficial to deep, so tasks should be sequenced intentionally in a way that enables increasingly substantive comprehension.

- **Practice and learning need to be *differentiated*:** Students need to be able to access tasks in different ways.

- **Practice and learning need to be *distributed*:** It needs to occur over multiple days, in multiple ways, to stick.

To be clear, this is not a call to eliminate either lessons or units; rather, I'm advocating for planning—both across months and within days—that reflects how people learn and apply complex skills and concepts. This planning might include individual lessons or several week units, sure. It may also include a week or month of project-based learning, a three-day problem-based approach around an essential question, or two weeks of independent reading to prepare for these sorts of inquiry-centered approaches. In short, the demands of the conceptual understanding that students need to gain should dictate instructional time, not the other way around. Chapters 1 (page 13) and 2 (page 39) go into this in more detail.

Where Rigor Begins: How to Use This Book

The remainder of *Ambitious Instruction: Teaching With Rigor in the Secondary Classroom* is organized for action in your classroom and at your school—your tasks and texts, of course, but also the collaboration and learning processes necessary to enhance and sustain them. Teachers, expect to find step-by-step blueprints of planning and pedagogical practices every step of the way; instructional leaders, know that every chapter breaks down key teaching and learning concepts and provides guidance on how teachers can collaborate on—in professional learning communities, with an instructional coach—and enact ambitious instructional practice. Examples from across the content areas are included throughout.

Chapters 1 and 2 act as a close-knit pair with the aim to get you rigor ready—that is, I discuss how to *plan* ambitious instruction. With a focus on rigorous performance assessments and texts, and a fresh view on planning, here's where you'll learn how to refine and sequence your curricula over the course of a school year.

Chapter 3 gets granular. You'll learn how to build the tasks necessary to power ambitious instruction on the daily. Here you'll find out ways to structure and sequence daily instruction that enables inquiry and supports students' ability to problem solve and argue.

Chapter 4 dives into facilitating rigorous learning, with a focus on launching and sustaining inquiry. Here you'll learn how to engage students during investigations of texts and interactive argumentation—that is, how to push student thinking toward the higher levels of intellectual development we'll discuss in this chapter.

Chapter 5 provides a comprehensive agenda for both personal and schoolwide professional development that you can use to learn to take up the work in planning and daily instruction.

To help you determine your entry point for changing insight into action, each chapter grounds you in the fundamentals and foundations of knowing, doing, and leading ambitious instruction, including what to look for and expect in students' intellectual work, how to plan and facilitate instruction to support this intellectual work, and how to design professional development to improve both. I also identify opportunities throughout to jump in and get started on the work with additional direction and inspiration. Each chapter concludes with a section titled The Big Idea, which summarizes its key takeaways that you can use as talking points for your review and means of introducing ambitious instruction to others.

One Last Word Before We Begin

If you're like me, you've become accustomed—perhaps even desensitized—to how books on curriculum and instruction work: a catchy acronym here, a step-by-step process there, a bunch of graphic organizer templates in the back. In the decades since the concept of backward design became popular, the approach has been tried countless times: the promise of the perfect process or the perfect planning template to solve our curriculum challenges.

Spoiler alert: they don't exist.

That's because a book can't solve teachers' planning challenges. What it can do is position teachers to develop solutions. Process, in other words, doesn't create rigor; it just supports *you* to create rigor. Process lives best in professional learning environments where you can learn through inquiry, analysis and enactment of your curriculum products, careful study of the texts and tasks, and collaborative planning around standards. Process lives or dies based on you—your thinking, your collaboration, your interests and orientations—and not templates.

This book, if you haven't already noticed, has a slant. It is not an exhaustive attempt at covering the whole of instruction. It does not purport to be the answer to every day of instruction in your classroom. What it does is leverage the results of key research to conceptualize and codify a kind of instruction that, if implemented regularly, can significantly impact students' ability to read, write, and think within and across disciplines.

Again, keep in mind that what follows is not a definitive vision of teaching; it may and should lead to more questions as you plan and implement—that's inquiry, after all. Inquiry is what to aim for and around. Approach these chapters as opportunities to experiment and learn from your work, to test and uncover. Aim for integration, too. Look for ways the principles and practices in this book can refine and enhance existing instruction, rather than erase it.

Opportunities and constraints surrounding rigor are the same as they have always been. Many schools—including, perhaps, your own—have focused or are focusing on rigor; many schools fail, often because they fail to build buy-in for doing the work in the first place. In the end, and especially at the start, it's less about what teachers know and can do instructionally and much more about belief and mindset—that this approach is worth teachers' time and effort, and that students can do this level of work. Building consensus regarding the effort and developing a common language and approach for doing so is critical to meaningfully changing your school's instructional core. Because while the challenges of supporting struggling learners are very real, teachers don't have a choice: the Common Core and other next generation college- and career-ready frameworks make it clear that *all* students are expected to learn and be proficient in, say, developing evidence-based arguments from the reading and analysis of multiple sources. This cannot be argued. Rather than seeing such competency as some level to reach, or beyond the current capacity of our students, we need to see the learning of it as the *means* to help students achieve proficiency and be college ready. We need to believe it is the core of our work.

And that is why it is the core of this book.

Getting Started on Ambitious Instruction: Building Curriculum Around Problems

A friend's late father was an avowed Francophile who, in the age before the internet and social media, was known among his circles as the authority on all things France. Friends and relatives called him all the time for advice on hotels, restaurants, and culture—so much so that he eventually was badgered into publishing a semiannual newsletter on his latest recommendations. That lasted more than two decades.

How did he come to be not only an expert but an authority on his subject area? Beyond simply his exposure to the content—he took two or three trips to France yearly—was his very specific approach to traveling, one that positioned him to be a learner, not just a tourist. Research was important, of course. He would go to his local library to read travel articles from *The New York Times*, the latest guidebooks on Paris, and so forth. But what I continue to marvel at, and the reason why I share this anecdote, was what he did *during* the trips. Every day he would set out to a different neighborhood and try to solve his investigation of the day: *Where should I eat dinner?* He would amble about the neighborhood, reviewing menus and talking to those in the community about where they ate; he would go into restaurants and chat up the proprietors, inquiring about ingredients and preparation and service to discern whether it met his standard. When he found one that did, he ate there.

I never met the man, but I'm not surprised he was viewed as almost never wrong on matters of food. And that's not because of good taste. It's because he had such a surefire process to build expertise—or, at least, know more than other people. There's no magic in his methods: he consciously and consistently built background knowledge, pursued questions through inquiry-based practices, sought the input and collaboration of others, and assessed his findings and ideas based on a set of criteria. It was, in a word, a rigorous way of figuring out what and where to eat.

Beyond being a cute anecdote, what this story exemplifies for me is the underlying spirit of ambitious instruction—*blatant curiosity*. People who are experts at what they do are passionate and knowledgeable about their subject matter, sure, but they are so because they are pursuing with purpose answers or solutions to that knowledge area; they work at that passion and knowing. Blatant curiosity. Blatant because it is designed, structured, educative, and intentional, and curiosity because interest and investment motivate and sustain learners, ensuring they become doers. Necessary in secondary classrooms is an intentional mix of thorough tasks that drive student engagement (curiosity) and well-thought-out capital-T teaching—modeling, an intentional sequence of activities, and feedback in the moment—to ensure students can engage in increasingly rigorous and independent ways (blatant).

Blatant curiosity is our driver in this chapter and the next as we focus on planning. The focus of this chapter is on the two tenets, (1) problem-based learning and (2) synthesis, that underlie the design of ambitious instruction, from the biggest semester-level project or paper to the smallest daily activity; you'll also learn how to start crafting problems for these big and small activities. Chapter 2 continues this focus by explaining how to put those principles in motion at the performance assessment, unit, and task levels of specificity. The purpose is simple: once you see what underlies rigor in and across content, you can more readily plan for it at the summative, unit, and daily levels.

Delving Into the Two Tenets

Inquiry-based instruction is hard. I say that at the outset of a section devoted to unpacking how to do it so that it's clear that the entry points I discuss in this chapter are just that; they're not meant to be exhaustive when it comes to planning and enacting this kind of work. But get to truly know and live these two tenets, and the 150 other things we do and say in rich classroom instruction will begin to reveal themselves.

Ambitious instruction is problem based. At the core of ambitious instruction is a rigorous and relevant problem—the kind that engages students in repeated opportunities to learn, apply, and expand content knowledge and skills. Problems are often framed as questions, but they are not merely questions; they are, more broadly, *opportunities* for sustained investigations into the same kind of issues with which professionals in the subject area or the general public wrestle.

Ambitious instruction involves, facilitates, and leads to synthesis. I use *synthesis* here broadly to reflect the combining of multiple content resources and modalities to facilitate inquiry; it also refers to the product or outcome of student learning when they do such tasks—that is, that students are integrating and synthesizing these multiple touchpoints to create their own arguments or draw their own conclusions.

Synthesis demands problems that encourage students to draw on multiple tools and perspectives to reach solutions or consensus; problems rely on synthesis to provide the content and learning processes necessary to sustain inquiry. Together, you've got the blueprint for ambitious instruction. Let's take a closer look at both problem-based learning and synthesis.

Ambitious Instruction Is Problem Based

Every discipline has problems.

That is, content areas have burning issues, questions, conflicts, and so on that define the subject and drive the work of professionals within it—historians, scientists, researchers, writers, critics, and so on. In other words, content areas have problems. In the study of literature, problems are often referred to as *puzzles*—contexts, patterns, strange or contradictory features, and more that suggest deeper meaning or intention beyond the literal level (Rainey, 2015). In the study of history, problems are posed as *central historical questions*—the key lingering questions or points of debate around the significant events, people, and issues of a given historical phenomenon or period (Caron, 2005; Reisman, 2012). In the study of science, in which the method of inquiry has long been codified, there are *research questions*—inquiries into unknown or contested phenomena in order to determine their forms, behavior, and relationships with other phenomena. You get the idea: each discipline has its own problem-framing language and devices.

Disciplines, in other words, are built on problems. These problems are central to doing the work of the discipline. Problems, because they are not yet (re)solved, shape what matters in a given discipline. They guide scholars and professionals of that discipline in choosing what to study and how to study it. Their sheer state as questions, issues, or dilemmas, with possible and possibly important solutions and implications, make the pursuit meaningful. Problems nag; they want to be solved. Disciplinarians take a personal and professional interest in pursuing their solutions— they are passionate about discovering them. As a result, the pursuit becomes relevant to the rest of their field and the world. Think of the great theories and wonderment about the dynamics of the physical universe, our seemingly ceaseless interest in the beliefs and values of the Founding Fathers, the continued intrigue and relevance of Shakespeare's figurative language, and so on. Tens of thousands of books and articles have been written about these examples. Everything there is to be said about them, it would seem, has been said. And yet, dozens of new contributions appear each year in well-traveled subject areas. The same concepts, the same problems, continue to produce new knowledge.

Meaningful problems, then, aren't simply solved. They are opportunities to extend and expand. Knowledge begets knowledge. When we interact with significant problems and the existing knowledge base on them, we generate new questions, theories, solutions. Perhaps more important, when we attend to these problems—whether individually or in collaboration with others—we bring our unique backgrounds and perspectives to bear on evidence, creating new evidence and new perspectives. Problems, in short, enable more than just knowledge and content areas; they enable people.

That includes your students. The problem-centered curriculum, one in which the most meaningful and engaging questions of the field or discipline guide the course of study, positions students to engage in rigorous content study and to take a personal interest in exploring the ideas of your content area in relation to their own ideas—doing synthesis, in other words. Your learning standards, believe it or not, have a lot to say about problems, too. As the sample standards in table 1.1 make clear, the Common Core, discipline-specific frameworks like the College, Career, and Civic Life (C3) Framework, and state standards like the Texas Essential Knowledge and Skills (TEKS) conceptualize the work of synthesis as inextricably linked to problem formation and solution in all disciplines.

Drawing from the standards in the table, the work of all disciplines is to solve problems by integrating, evaluating, and synthesizing multiple sources of information; these occur in and through inquiry and investigation. Problems—and problem solving—initiate and facilitate this work; they are teaching tools. As this chapter and the next demonstrate, they determine what students will solve and how they will perform, the texts and resources they will draw upon to solve said problems, and the literacy practices necessary to support student engagement throughout the problem-solving process. Start here, it might be said, and you can go anywhere with your instruction.

You may have ascertained that problems can be *essential questions* (Wiggins & McTighe, 2005), overarching questions that guide a unit—if not a semester or year—of study, or *guiding questions*, which address a very specific piece of knowledge or skill within a single or few lessons of instruction. Unlike essential questions, however, which tend to address broad conceptual understanding (for example, *What*

Table 1.1: Examples of Problem Formation and Problem Solving Addressed in State and National Standards

Common Core	C3 Framework	TEKS
Integrate and evaluate multiple sources of information presented in different media or formats (e.g., visually, quantitatively) as well as in words in order to address a question or solve a problem. (RI.11–12.7 for ELA, Social Studies, and Science)	Assess their individual and collective capacities to take action to address local, regional, and global problems, taking into account a range of possible levers of power, strategies, and potential outcomes. (Middle School; D4.7.6–8)	Use a problem-solving and decision-making process to identify a problem, gather information, list and consider options, consider advantages and disadvantages, choose and implement a solution, and evaluate the effectiveness of the solution. (Middle School; 7.113.19)
Integrate multiple sources of information presented in diverse formats and media (e.g., visually, quantitatively, orally) in order to make informed decisions and solve problems, evaluating the credibility and accuracy of each source and noting any discrepancies among the data. (SL.11–12.2 for ELA, Social Studies, and Science)	Use disciplinary and interdisciplinary lenses to understand the characteristics and causes of local, regional, and global problems; instances of such problems in multiple contexts; and challenges and opportunities faced by those trying to address these problems over time and place. (High School; D4.6.9–12)	Apply social studies methodologies encompassing a variety of research and analytical tools to explore questions or issues thoroughly and fairly to include multiple perspectives. (High School; 9–12.113.47)
Conduct short as well as more sustained research projects to answer a question (including a self-generated question) or solve a problem; narrow or broaden the inquiry when appropriate; synthesize multiple sources on the subject, demonstrating understanding of the subject under investigation. (W.11–12.7 for ELA, Social Studies, and Science)	Evaluate citizens' and institutions' effectiveness in addressing social and political problems at the local, state, tribal, national, and/or international level. (High School; D2.Civ.5.9–12)	

Source for standards: National Council for the Social Studies [NCSS], 2013; NGA & CCSSO, 2010; Texas Education Agency, n.d.

is history?), problems attend to key content concerns, enabling learners to see how disciplinary experts formulate and respond to such concerns (Moje, 2015). Unlike guiding questions, which tend to address the specific content knowledge students are to know on a given day (for example, *What informs inheritance?*), problems emphasize the analytical and argumentative aspects of the given topic. Problems, in short, are multiday, multiweek explorations by design—they need and are worth that time.

It may at first seem superfluous or tedious to add an additional category of instruction-guiding questions, but such a step is necessary if we mean to sustain deep learning over time and set our instruction up to meaningfully pursue inquiry, both necessary for synthesis. Many teachers construct essential questions to guide their curriculum or the act of planning itself, but often the resulting essential questions themselves aren't all that essential for students to answer. In fact, students often do not answer them at all. This is because essential questions are often framed at such a broad level as to serve as a kind of snapshot or representation of the topic or discipline as a whole (for example, *What social opportunities and problems arise from an interconnected global economy?*), thus making it difficult to respond to in daily instruction or even a unit-ending summative assessment. Even when teachers directly assess the question, they often do not ask students to do so in ways commensurate with the complexity of the question and length of time studying it. With a problem, however, the focus is specifically on supporting students to answer, to use the problem-solving process as a means of developing the conceptual understanding of the given discipline. Problems are, essentially, mini–essential questions supported by instruction, activities, and questioning (investigations) that set students up to connect and respond to the overarching questions of your courses.

Bad problems are easy to spot—you've seen enough of them on everything from units online to standardized testing, after all. They're artificial; they don't address topics or issues authentic to either the content or students' own lives. There's no palpable excitement or interest—from student or teacher—in solving them; they feel like schoolwork. They don't encourage genuine reasoning and thoughtful writing. Students complete the work but don't develop significant conceptual understanding and skills (Journell, Friedman, Thacker, & Fitchett, 2018).

Good problems are different. They inspire curiosity, engagement, and even passion; they are, as Elizabeth Birr Moje (2015) notes, action oriented. They're distinguished, in my experience, by three traits.

1. **They are relevant:** Relevant problems serve multiple masters. They reflect key problems of the content area (albeit adapted or made accessible to secondary students), align with course goals or themes, and connect to students' lives in and out of school; they mean something to study and solve.

2. **They are arguable:** Arguable problems are not just debatable, though that is important; rather, a range of possible responses to the problem are not simply possible but likely, and students will be challenged by their peers to provide the evidence and reasoning in support of those positions. It means something, in other words, to take a stance on the problem, and it

requires some thoughtfulness in developing that response. Good problems encourage and develop this thoughtfulness.

3. **They are sophisticated:** Sophisticated problems encourage inference or interpretation; they demand more than simple pro-or-con responses but consideration of both the underlying beliefs and values of the issues and the patterns across responses to them. They require time and discussion to figure out, sustaining inquiry and ultimately leading to representation of understanding in new and more complex forms.

Figure 1.1 provides examples of bad and good problems in the areas of English, social studies, and science. Note the use of the dreaded cellphone prompt, the writing task that launched a thousand bad state tests: its superior rewrite, listed in the corresponding column, increases the relevance, argumentativeness, and sophistication of the task by moving away from simplistic pro-or-con perspectives and toward the formulation of a specific proposal in response to human interaction (that is, the communication) rather than the technology (that is, the cellphones). The social studies comparison, too, shows a marked improvement across multiple levels. The initial problem, a common essay question in high school social studies coursework, is reductive, asking students to choose one cause when the history of a nation, especially the United States', is complex and multicausal. A more sophisticated and arguable approach, as dictated in the corresponding problem, is to consider the causality as part of an evaluation of both the specific events in the run-up to the war and the broader narrative of American history, taking a stance on whether war was avoidable.

	Sample Bad Problem	**Sample Good Problem**
ELA	Should cellphones be banned in schools?	What role should high schools take in managing the personal communication of its students?
Social Studies	What was the primary cause of the Civil War?	Was the Civil War inevitable?
Science	How are characteristics of one generation passed to the next?	Is biology destiny?

Figure 1.1: Comparing good and bad problems across content areas.

The changes evident in figure 1.1 are not accidental; rather, the questions emphasize relevance, argumentation, and sophistication in improving what students are asked to know and do. To enhance argumentation, an intentional effort was made in each revision to avoid reductive thinking—not narrowing perspectives or responses down to a single or few choices (for example, primary causes of the Civil War or whether or not cellphones should be banned) but positioning students to develop the stance or solution (for example, *What role . . . ?*) themselves. To enhance sophistication, look to the underlying issues—not simple matters of causality or pro-or-con but deeper inquiries into the kinds of actions and outcomes and the extent to which they can be controlled. Finally, to enhance relevance, focus on making problems engaging—not merely arguable but *worth* arguing, emphasizing the core ideas of the discipline (for example, the nature versus nurture debate in the life and psychological sciences) and positioning students to respond significantly to significant issues.

As figure 1.1 (page 19) suggests, good problems not only have certain qualities but also take on certain forms, which are identifiable and can be developed and enacted with intention in order to support student learning of content and skill. Such problems orient students toward seeing content knowledge acquisition as problem oriented in nature and content as something to be understood, challenged, and solved. Such problems demand content-specific intellectual tools and instructional supports to solve sophisticated, rigorous, and inquiry-based problems—conducting experiments and investigations in science, analyzing primary sources in social studies, and close reading literary texts and criticism in ELA. Such problems could, therefore, be powerful instructional tools to both position students to demonstrate their developing understanding of content and argument and support the guiding process of learning it.

But not all problems are the same. I have found that teachers need a variety of problems that serve the curriculum and support deep content and skill learning in the content area; that attend to the rhetoric and conceptual concerns articulated in the state's standards; that are reflective of the problems faced and posed by expert practitioners; and that are relevant, argumentative, and sophisticated. Problem formation and use, then, will need to be intentional.

By being mindful of the three problem types described in this section—(1) intellectual, (2) interpretive, and (3) issue (Cawn, 2016)—you can diversify the problems you develop.

Intellectual Problems

Intellectual problems address the significant underlying tensions of your discipline: the ideas and philosophies and principles about what people believe, how society should function, what matters or counts as truth in your area of study, and so on. Unlike issue problems, in which the goal is to propose or assess solutions, intellectual problems often address the conceptual, philosophical, and moral dilemmas at play in the topics and texts of your subject matter—in other words, they address the problems that arise when we try to solve the issue. The intellectual problem of what it means to be a post-racial society, for instance, was not an expected or desired outcome of the politics, policy, and interpersonal relationships stemming from the Civil Rights Movement; our present state, the result of several complex events and factors, poses several challenges and unknowns. That is not to say that such an intellectual problem cannot be solved or resolved—we can define what *post-racial* is, consider its implications, propose ways of attending to its challenges, and so forth—but those possible definitions and solutions are many, complex, and prone to critique.

That intellectual problems should arise when our thought processes and belief systems run into conflicts and dilemmas, and that they should actively encourage dialogue and disagreement, is exactly why they are so powerful to their given fields and as teaching tools in your classroom. Intellectual problems call for hypotheses and interpretations; they prompt discussion and debate. They do not merely linger but serve as the defining problems of the discipline: ideas about the meaning of life and how to live it in English language arts; the causes and effects of actors and events, as well as conceptions of progress, in social studies; or the explanations, possibilities, and limitations of the known physical universe in the sciences.

To engage in such meanings requires problems that get at the abstract or contested nature of a topic or issue, and thus intellectual problems can be classified further into two types: (1) problems of *definition* and (2) problems of *evaluation*. Problems of definition involve clarifying the meaning of a concept that is complex and may mean different things in different contexts or to different people. The earlier problem of what it means to be a "post-racial society," for instance, is a concept without clear or consensus definition; so, too, is the question of what privacy means in the digital age. In either of these cases, students might consult an array of resources—from contemporary texts that directly reference the problem to historical texts, such as foundational documents (for example, the Constitution), that merely allude to it—to develop possible meanings. It is likely that a range of possible and conflicting perspectives on what each concept means and what those meanings entail will arise.

Evaluation problems ask students to assess the value or validity of phenomena. In this case, the meaning of the idea or issue in question is clear; the intellectual debate is over whether it is true or effective. The problem *Is Gatsby great?* (Fitzgerald, 1925), for instance, prompts students to judge the merits of a particular character. Is the title of the novel ironic, or is the book, in fact, arguing that readers should aspire to Gatsby's pursuits and worldview? Problems of evaluation work to position students to join ongoing and significant content-area debates. They provide the frame of the claim, and students work within it and expand its meaning and possibility. For example, the question *How revolutionary was the Revolutionary War?* positions the historical event in relation to its potential radicalism; students join the conversation by taking up claims on the degree to which it is relevant.

Researchers have repeatedly referred to attending to the ambiguity and complexity of subject matter as the core conceptual development area of late high school and postsecondary (Chall, 1983; Perry, 1999). At the grades 11–12 level, the Common Core, the C3 Framework, and other learning benchmarks repeatedly articulate the necessity in all subject areas for students to ascertain and respond to uncertain and conflicting information. Our goal, then, should be to regularly "problematize" issues as intellectual matters—as not having simple or readily available resolutions, and as requiring deeper investigation of content-area texts in order to define, compare, and assess key concepts and perspectives. These kinds of problems should be front and center in content-area inquiry—in fact, they're the kind that encourage meaningful inquiry or ensure it can take place.

Interpretive Problems

When a text is complex, it has both a surface meaning (what it literally says) and a subtext (the rhetorical or conceptual underpinnings that convey significance or affect readers). Interpretive problems address this subtext. In such cases, the words on the page alone are not sufficient for readers to grasp the full meaning or implications of the text's message: the words and ideas are "problematic," and readers must interpret them through close reading of specific portions of the text, comparing or connecting them with other evidence, and considering the context—their own and the author's—in which it was written.

Interpretive problems, then, are about how a text has meaning—how ideas, organization, and language work to express meaning—and what this means for the reader and for the author. Texts have meaning through the themes or key ideas they convey; the effect they have on the logic and emotion of the reader; the intent its author or authors attempt to realize, and how they communicate that intent through their organization of the text (for example, structure or plot); and the role of the specific language in the text in relation to the meaning (Goldman, McCarthy, & Burkett, 2015). Determining the meaning and use of a symbol: interpretive. Determining how the organization of an argument makes it more or less persuasive: interpretive. Considering the implications or applications of language in a new or different context: interpretive.

All disciplines and fields have interpretive problems. In law, the wording of a statute or precedent is picked over and analyzed closely in order to understand its meanings, applications, and implications in particular settings. In theology, religious scholars examine the specific language of a sacred text—say, the Bible or the Koran—and try to parse out what words and phrases mean, what that language meant at the time of its composition, and the implications for how the faithful should practice. For scholars of literature, the study of fiction often involves pursuing the symbolic and thematic layer of meaning underlying the narrative and language of the text. Even our daily lives are punctuated by problems of interpretation: a confusing text message, that surprise twist at the end of the movie, that ingredient in an appetizer that you can't quite place (Cilantro? Mayonnaise? Fish sauce?).

A parsing of the preceding examples suggests that we can use interpretive problems to address two things: (1) the meaning of some aspect of a text or texts or (2) the effect or significance of that meaning; teachers should attend to both. Problems of *meaning* occur when key language or concepts represent new, unfamiliar, or implicit messages—think of connotations, figurative language, abstract nouns, and so forth. What the second amendment of the Constitution is saying about the right to bear arms, for instance, requires us to look carefully at the use of language—if not punctuation—to suggest what the law means. The repeated appearance of the green light in *The Great Gatsby* (Fitzgerald, 1925) requires students to consider what it means in relation to the titular character and to that which he and America pursue. Problems of *effect or significance*, on the other hand, consider how the author's choices translate to or influence the audience interacting with the text. For instance, students might be asked to consider why the Founding Fathers chose to use certain language (for example, the word *inalienable*) and how such choices affected audiences at the time or how they affect them now. With *Gatsby,* students might be asked to consider how the reappearance of the green light at the novel's end signals the key ideas of the novel, and how the descriptive language of that ending works to emotionally affect the reader. The Common Core college and career readiness anchor standards (CCRA) repeatedly address these two interpretive problem subtypes. The standards call for students to trace the development of central idea or theme (CCRA.R.2) and language use (CCRA.R.4) over the course of the text, and to define the use of figurative and connotative language (CCRA.L.3). Furthermore, students are also expected to articulate the rhetorical and aesthetic effects of word choice (CCRA.L.4), syntax and structure (CCRA.L.5), and point of view (CCRA.R.6; NGA & CCSSO, 2010).

In short, solving interpretive problems involves constructing inferences that respond to and expand upon the language of the text; such inferences are derived from the text but not limited to it (Goldman et al., 2015). To make such interpretations, students must synthesize what the text says and their prior knowledge and experiences, including their understanding of text structures, rhetorical situations, and the perspectives and beliefs of others (Lee, 2007). And to do that, students need to be positioned to see that your content-area texts contain signals that alert readers to interpretative problems, and to know which resources to draw upon to support analysis (Lee & Spratley, 2010). This is teachable, and we must teach it if students are to not only solve interpretive problems independently and proficiently but also value doing so.

Issue Problems

Every content area has pressing or persistent issues, the kind where the deepest moral, philosophical, and ideological concerns of the discipline intersect with current events or future applications that challenge these concerns. Issue problems position students as problem solvers of these concerns. Proposing or evaluating solutions to climate change in science, to American foreign policy problems in social studies, to school or community issues in English—all are examples of common issue problems in secondary classrooms.

Intellectual and issue problems appear to be similar but are distinguished by what they ask students to do. The former asks students to define, analyze, or evaluate the meaning or significance of a concept while the latter asks students to construct or respond to ideas about the best solutions to a given issue. An intellectual problem on the subject of climate change, for instance, might ask, *Are industrial superpowers like China or the United States responsible for negative effects of climate change on smaller economies?* An issue problem might ask students to consider, *What can the United States do to lead on climate change solutions?* In our two examples, the intellectual problem asks students to weigh the relationship between a nation's size and economic and environmental impact and its potential responsibility to other nations when addressing the potential implications of that impact, and the issue problem asks students to propose action. They may potentially utilize the relationship between concepts as support, but the main goal is to make a recommendation.

Issue problems typically feature use of *can* or *should* in the problem formation—a sign that students are expected to propose or evaluate a recommendation. We can typically put them in two categories. First, *proposal* issue problems leave the solution generation to students: arguing for a homework policy, suggesting changes to federal policy, proposing a particular design or schematic for an engineering challenge, and so on. And second, *evaluation* issue problems provide the proposed solution, asking students to respond to the validity of the proposal: the worth of adopting a specific homework policy, the impact of a policy (for example, the Affordable Care Act), or the quality of a design proposal. Because they provide students with an initial or common claim on a given issue, evaluation issue problems make useful scaffolding tools during the study of topics and texts, an entry into developing conceptual understanding and meaningful perspectives on the issues. Because they require students to generate original ideas or solutions, proposal issue problems make useful summative assessments or projects, an opportunity to synthesize understanding of texts and topics into a complete representation or response.

Because they appear so frequently on standardized testing (for example, the cellphone prompt, see page 19), we often presume issue problems to be exemplars of what formal argumentative essays should ask and look like. Just because a task prompts a position, evaluation, or resolution, however, does not mean it is sophisticated. Effectiveness depends on the degree to which students are encouraged and enabled to take on more sophisticated positions. The testing company ACT, which administers the titular college admissions exam, recognized as much when it changed its writing assessment, a project I consulted on. The assessment changed from what was once an overly reductive pro-or-con evaluation issue problem (for example, *Should schools enforce a dress code?*) to an assessment construct that includes both evaluation and proposal issue problems; the updated test asks students to "analyze the relationship between [their] perspective and at least one other perspective" and "develop and support [their] ideas with reasoning and examples" (ACT, n.d.). Such a change represents not merely an increase in rigor but a significant increase in responsibility and opportunity for students to develop coherent and novel responses; our use of issue problems throughout the curriculum must do the same.

Table 1.2 summarizes the three problem types.

Table 1.2: Summary of Problem Types

Problem Type and Subtype		What We Expect Learners to Do	Example
Intellectual	Definition	Clarify the meaning in a complex context.	*What should count as* truth?
	Evaluation	Assess the validity of perspectives.	*How should history view the Soviet Union?* (see next chapter, page 39)
Interpretive	Meaning	Define the inferred meaning or implications.	*What does the Second Amendment actually mean in terms of the right to bear arms?*
	Effect or significance	Analyze how rhetoric is used to effectively articulate ideas.	*How does E. B. White (1999) use syntax in "Ring of Time" to convey his impressions of youth?*
Issue	Proposal	Generate a solution or perspective.	*What would be an effective approach to curtail e-cigarette usage among teens?*
	Evaluation	Assess the relevance and value of a solution or perspective.	*How effective have the FDA's efforts to curtail e-cigarette usage among teens been?*

Ready to try creating your own problems? See Developing High-Quality Problems (page 28) later in this chapter for a detailed problem-generating process.

Ambitious Instruction Involves, Facilitates, and Leads to Synthesis

Problems enable synthesis. Pursuing answers to a problem demands careful study of texts and research. Problems lead to analysis and interpretation, which leads to answers. Most important, problems lead to understanding. Problems spur the process of inquiry—of considering multiple perspectives and weighing possible responses—and thus evoke our own perspectives. We respond to the problem because we know or believe something, and in developing a response, we learn how we know. The problem-formation process found later in this chapter attests to that.

To synthesize is to generate new ideas from the review, assessment, and adaptation of existing elements. In the language of Bloom's (1956) taxonomy of cognitive rigor, synthesis connotes the formation of a conclusion by considering or combining previous ones. Bloom's taxonomy considers synthesis the second-highest order of cognitive rigor (though a later, revised version of the taxonomy [Anderson & Krathwohl, 2001] bumps it up to the top level, under the category of Create). It is also the most cognitively rigorous of task types in Webb's (1997) Depth of Knowledge, known there as *extended thinking*. Definitions of synthesis commonly articulate it as representing unity, complexity, totality (Synthesis, n.d.a, n.d.b); in the context of teaching, I often hear the word used synonymously with *propose, integrate, arrange*, and so on. Synthesis is both something whole, understanding drawn from a combination of many elements, and something new, understanding represented in the form of a different perspective, form or medium, or depth and intensity.

If all this makes synthesis appear more like a multifaceted, all-encompassing learning component than a rare and infrequently taught thinking skill, that's because it is and should be. Think about how often you synthesize in both your personal and professional life. You use student learning artifacts—be it students' written work or your observations—to determine subsequent lesson plans. You draw conclusions and ideas about your life and that of others from what you read about in the news or from what you hear or see in the people in your life. That same frequency, intensity, and automaticity that go into your generative thinking should also be true of what you ask students to do in your classroom.

The good news is it's easier and more practical than you might think to make it happen. As figure 1.2 shows, synthesis can be represented and realized in multiple forms, from the more tangible (like coming up with solutions to an issue problem) to the more theoretical (like making a claim in response to an interpretive problem). Thinking and activities on the other side of the matrix, such as generating observations, should be viewed as *supporting* synthesis, not in opposition to it. Note, too, the relationship between synthesis and analysis: complementary but not synonymous.

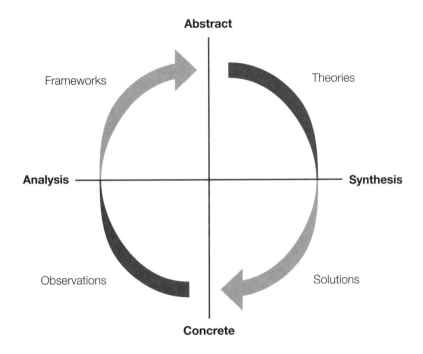

Figure 1.2: Synthesis similarity matrix.

Analysis is what we do to understand and represent information; synthesis is applying that understanding to create new knowledge (that is, theories or solutions). Analysis requires us to compare, delineate, and define—hence why it results in observations and frameworks and the like. Synthesis encourages us to project, hypothesize, integrate—hence why it results in new representations of knowing.

In this book, and for the purposes of teaching, these forms of synthesis are realized through the solving of challenging content-area problems. Synthesis already has some stature in the teaching and learning lexicon. The Advanced Placement (AP) English Language and Composition exam has a synthesis essay task, which prompts students to "synthesize information from a variety of sources to inform their own discussion of a topic" (College Board, n.d.). Many college composition courses, not to mention publishers of college composition readers, refer to a specific kind of formal academic writing assignment by the same name (Segev-Miller, 2007); others estimate that more than 80 percent of tasks assigned in college involve reading and responding to sources (Nist & Simpson, 2000). This response requires synthesis.

But synthesis just as well refers to common instances of teaching and learning across the content areas. What would you call students comparing data garnered from a lab experiment with the results from another study in order to develop a hypothesis about the phenomena observed? Synthesis. What about reviewing cases or examples of attempts to solve a school or community problem in order to compose a solution of one's own? Synthesis. Analyzing and evaluating several historians' perspectives in order to determine what caused the Civil War? Synthesis.

We associate the concept of inquiry as synonymous with synthesis because, well, synthesis *is* inquiry. Both refer to solving significant academic problems through exploration of ideas and evidence; both involve proposing and testing hypotheses, considering evidence, and developing understanding and positions through dialogue and writing. When you teach students how to synthesize and give them rigorous tasks that prompt them to apply critical-thinking skills, you're doing inquiry-based instruction.

While synthesis remains one of the higher-order-thinking skills teachers aspire to address, like evaluation and analysis, it remains nebulous to students, if not to teachers. It's hard to make accessible in instruction and instructional language. Teachers are further challenged to fit it all in. We want to encourage and enable critical thinking, but we fret over all the things students should know first before they engage in acts of deep thinking. *Comprehension before critique*, a common saying reminds us. Critical thinking is positioned as a culmination of learning, rather than the process by which students learn. It is rarely addressed in full or directly.

Where it is missing, where it is needed most, is in daily instruction. Yes, that's right. Rather than making the highest-order thinking infrequent and summative—the stuff of projects or end assessments—it should be the whole of instruction. Positioning synthesis as both the process and product of our teaching means not having to choose between comprehension and critical thinking; it prioritizes both. In synthesis, we understand to argue; comprehension supports critical thinking. Our own common core as teachers should be capital-T teaching students how to do it.

Developing High-Quality Problems

The two tenets, problem-based learning and synthesis, can feel a little, well, fuzzy at the conceptual level. It really helps to see their practical applications *in* practice, particularly when planning. Think of problems as your signpost for where you begin and where you'll end up. You'll know you've achieved your learning outcomes if students can solve the problems you give them. Think of synthesis as telling you about what you need in terms of the depth of students' responses. It also tells you what the intellectual work should be to reach that depth. You need only build out the curricular products to support it.

Problems are all around us, but they don't just come from anywhere; we derive them, with the specific intention of serving content and skill learning. That means you must be deliberate about creating problems, developing and positioning them as supports for students. Set the problem up carefully to guide teaching and student learning, because it must anchor instruction.

Anchoring means said problems must get at or spark what is essential to know and do in your course and content area. It also may mean breaking a bad habit. In the initial years of Common Core–era professional development and curriculum design, it was not uncommon to find teachers being told to translate the language of standards into essential questions, and then to build significant instructional plans around them. For example, Common Core Writing anchor standard one, the standard articulating that students should compose formal written arguments (NGA & CCSSO, 2010), became the essential question What is an argument?, which became a dedicated unit on argumentation. Of course, students need to know what an argument is, but how can they ever do so meaningfully without understanding what and how disciplinarians in your content area—historians, scientists, critics—argue? Literate practice is learned through, not around, content learning. Attempting to address only and explicitly the standards is not only insufficient but reductive, stripping the rigor and relevance of your teaching. Your problems, then, will need to be discipline specific, topical, and attentive to the core knowledge and ways of knowing the content under study. The skills that standards articulate serve to support the answer to this challenge. Maintaining the integrity of your teaching, and enhancing the intellectual work done in your classroom, means not unnecessarily separating content from skills; it means developing problems that support learning of both.

To do so requires attention to function (that is, the criteria established for good problems: relevance, argumentation, sophistication) and form (that is, the problem types: intellectual, interpretive, issue). The problem-formation process that I describe in the following sections incorporates both. In addition to describing the step and actions needed to complete it, I also include a bit about the step in action, with a description of how it informs the problems in a real curricular situation. In this case, I highlight a ninth-grade English class in an urban high school that was making the transition from fifty-minute daily instructional periods to a seventy-five-minute block occurring four days a week. Because the teachers I worked with had very real concerns about the attention and engagement levels of their students, we approached generating the problems as an issue problem itself. How might this school make the transition instructive, not only for teachers—who were studying how to teach in the block—but for students, too? As you'll see in some of the problems generated—*What does it take to adapt and grow as a learner in times or situations of change and challenge?*—the teachers sought to align opportunity with outcomes. We did this with two goals: (1) to develop problems that addressed both student interest or need and the broader school's goals and (2) to attend to the core content knowledge and skills necessary to succeed in high school.

Step 1: Anticipation—Establishing Relevance

Earlier in this chapter I introduced the idea of relevance as the degree to which a problem aligns with the core knowledge and skills of your content area, the goals and values of your school and community, and the students' interests and needs. Problem formation starts there. The good news is you're not starting from zero in these areas. In some form or another, those foundations and raw materials are already in place. Maybe you've organized your year or course (for example, by historical era in social studies or by topic or fundamental theorems in science) or you know the core ideas or questions of the content. Maybe you have some go-to texts and resources to use to address them. All of this can help guide you toward potential problems.

So, go there first: generate ideas by interacting with the materials themselves, such as your unit plans, your assessments, and so on. Such a pedagogical reading (Bain, 2012) can take any number of approaches: examining how the text or content addresses your standards (Alston & Barker, 2014) and using those areas to determine instructional focus; articulating learning goals as the source of determining instructional plans (Morris & Hiebert, 2011); or collaboratively reading and reviewing texts or content in order to address the key comprehension and critical-thinking components of the materials (Cawn, 2016). I recommend attending to all three: consider (1) the learning goals, (2) the core content knowledge, and (3) school and student needs already known or current. Consider how you can address all three inside a chunk of instruction. Given what your goals are and what is already in place, ask yourself the following questions.

- "What is the goal of this unit or plan of instruction, and how is it connected to core content and skill learning?"
- "What do students already know, should know by now, really need to know soon, and so on?"
- "What ideas in this content or unit are most worth responding to?"

This line of questioning aims to locate the sources or significance underlying a potential instructional problem—the kernel of the idea—rather than the problem itself; that will come.

Step 2: Formation—Finding the Argument

The idea is there; now it needs to take shape. With some key ideas, goals, and objectives in mind, zoom in on what's arguable. Look for aspects that enable multiple perspectives, requiring students to access multiple texts or resources to respond and encouraging them to generate new ideas from these sources (Kamil et al., 2008). Avoid the temptation to fall back on the typical sorts of essential questions such as those on naming or ordering factors or causes (for example, *What were causes of the Civil War?*, or *Why are some physical systems more stable than others?*). These questions may encourage multiple perspectives, sure, but in reinforcing those perspectives, they rarely enable students to demonstrate new understanding and new perspectives. Instead, start by thinking intentionally about performance. Given the learning goals, content, curriculum materials, and so on, what is it I really want students to know or do? The problem should frame and guide this thinking. Considering the shape of the problem through the lens of problem type can help. For example, which kind of problem, exactly, sets up the kind of thinking you want from your students about this content and skill? Consider those named key ideas against the possible purpose and pursuit of the problem. Is this the sort of knowing or doing that encourages or requires evaluation or definition of the meaning or effect of language or rhetoric? Does it encourage assessment or recommendation of an issue? The goal here is to orient yourself to the kind of intellectual work you want to guide students to do—binding the problem to a type helps frame the ideas the problem will articulate and attend to.

With the ninth-grade teachers in our example, they started codifying the problem by articulating the two lines of relevant inquiry established in their initial consideration of objectives, content, and context: (1) the big ideas and significance behind issues of schools, learning, and adolescents and (2) the possible goal setting or changes students themselves could articulate. The latter line of thinking felt promising to the teachers. It just made sense, given it was the first month of high school for these students, to prioritize goal setting and reflection. The first component, however, was trickier. It's tempting to problematize something around the multiple internal and external factors that influence a person—many an essential question does. But as we consider potential texts to address those factors—excerpts, say, from Paul Tough's (2012) *How Children Succeed* or Carol S. Dweck's (2006) *Mindset*—we should reconsider our purpose: that we are thinking about these texts so that we can ensure that students are aware of and act on certain factors (for example, character or mindsets), not so that they can argue whether they exist or not, nor to consider whether one has more influence than another. To make this potential problem arguable, we must realize that students will need to be able to connect with and expand the concepts in the potential texts—in other words, to take ideas which are not their own and make them personal and relevant to their own lives. One way to do so is to frame concepts like grit and mindset as intellectual problems to evaluate. That is, to ask, "Of what worth are these ideas in the complex reality of school and society?" There is plenty of chatter among social scientists on these matters already—seems like the perfect opportunity for students to ponder and respond to these practitioners, and to learn how to participate in the literate practices of your discipline.

Step 3: Articulation—Focusing on Sophistication

With an arguable concept in place for the problem, the next step is to determine how to articulate the problem in ways commensurate with what you expect students to know and do in response to it. Of course, the wording or framing of a task alone is no guarantee of improved student understanding, but research has shown it to significantly impact how and to what extent students respond (Nussbaum & Kardash, 2005; Wiley & Voss, 1999). It also influences how you perceive what students can and should be doing. So, while all the expected instructional supports—such as direct instruction, appropriate and relevant texts, activities, and others—are still to come, articulating a complex problem can play a meaningful role in determining those supports, giving them clarity and purpose.

Articulating a problem so that it sets students up to do meaningful intellectual work means attending carefully to the use of language in the question stem and how it might enable or disable student thinking—both in a summative response and formatively during the learning process. There is no single way to articulate a problem. It is essential to continually tweak and finesse the language so that it aligns with your purpose and expectations. Start by asking yourself, "What is a sophisticated viewpoint on the problem area, and to what extent does the problem as written enable it?" Consider, too, accessibility. Is the problem as articulated solvable for students while also being challenging or novel for them?

Try putting it on paper first, warts and all. Once you have articulated an initial draft of the problem, consider the range of possible student responses. In what ways can they respond given the language of the problem, and how are they likely to given that language? A strong, sophisticated problem has the following characteristics.

- **It cannot be easily answered:** Students cannot immediately or sufficiently answer without support; they will have to learn first about what or how to respond.

- **It requires responses that are not short or simple:** Students will need to draw from multiple pieces of evidence to develop claims; their responses, verbal or written, are likely to show evidence of working out a line of reasoning in process.

- **It prompts more than simply an opinion:** Students' connections, definitions, and analysis of significance or implications are more than evidence or reasoning in support of a claim; they are embedded in the claim itself.

Keep testing until the articulation meets these criteria.

Let's return to that potential problem previously noted as particularly tricky, that is, the big ideas and significance behind issues of schools, learning, and adolescents. We began with the idea of evaluating the concepts and issues that go into adolescent learning and development, like mindset and grit, for instance. The concept of grit seems particularly intriguing. Not only is grit connected to the power of character and individuality, it hits one of the most significant thematic and philosophical concerns of the world—the extent to which people have agency and free will in a world that is complex and often outside one's locus of control. Considering the relationship between this idea and the power and possibility of the whole person, school, or community offers an intriguing start to problem formation. You may ask your students to wonder, *Is grit alone sufficient to enable a student to learn and grow?* The question gives students an opportunity to zoom in on one aspect of their lives that they may not have previously considered, and to consider an aspect's relative weight juxtaposed to other individual and collective social and environmental concerns. However, singling out grit, making it the focus of student learning and response, may downplay the other concepts or aspects discussed across the unit. The question may also narrow or overly simplify students' responses to the simple yay-or-nay arguments we seek to avoid. *Is grit sufficient?* seems, then, like a really good single or multiday lesson (more on that soon). It would work better supporting a somewhat more expansive problem that allows students to consider and synthesize multiple perspectives—inclusive of, but not limited to, grit—and generate new understandings.

That problem, the ninth-grade teachers came to realize as they workshopped it in their learning community, should ask students to consider not just what will inform possible outcomes—because those factors are being established for students through the readings—but also what it takes, given grit and all sorts of other concerns, to produce more desirable outcomes. This idea of demands or needs dovetails nicely with the issue problem readily identified earlier, that of having students set a plan or strategy for themselves in order to support their learning and growth. In fact, analyzing and assessing the range of challenges sets students up to answer the issue problem. So, the teachers tried it out again: *What does it take to adapt and grow as a learner in times or situations of challenge?* Arguable? Yes, one could take multiple perspectives. Does it require the generation of new ideas from review of existing ones? Yes, students will need to synthesize knowledge gleaned from texts with personal experience and perspective to determine a response. Sophisticated? Yes, students will need to consider the role and weight of several factors—individual, social, environmental—to develop a line of argument. Requiring instructional supports? Yes, plenty of opportunities to teach students how to read texts on social science research, weigh various and potentially conflicting claims, and develop their own claims from multiple pieces of evidence.

Step 4: Expansion—Creating Investigations

The problem the ninth-grade teachers created, *What does it take to adapt and grow as a learner in times or situations of challenge?*, is too big to solve in a single lesson, or even in multiple lessons. Its very complexity and depth demand time, focus, exploration, and instruction in order to answer it. Students will need additional guidance to aid this exploration at the daily level—smaller problems that, if solved, will help guide students toward answering the major problem. For that reason, let's call such subproblems *investigations*.

Investigations are inquiry-based opportunities that help build understanding of and responses to a broader, unit-spanning problem and can be solved in a relatively short period of time—that is, in *one to five* lessons. Investigations may be about a single concept or text, or they may address a specific aspect of the broader problem. They have the same attributes of a good problem but are shorter and much more finite. The rejected problem from the previous step, *Is grit alone sufficient?*, is a good example of a potentially effective investigation question. It specifically addresses one component or concept of the problem, and positions students to build evidence about grit's role into an answer to the guiding problem. Another example is, *How do authors characterize adolescence, and are these characterizations accurate?*, a dual interpretive and intellectual problem that serves the purposes of providing opportunities to do rhetorical analysis and consider what portrayals of youth in text and media tell us—or don't tell us—about how to be. Interpretive problems work really well as investigations. They're often specific to a text or concept, and students can usually solve them within the span of a single or a few lessons.

Our goal with investigations is to stack and sequence these problems in an order that optimizes answering these questions and the overarching problem. Obviously, we cannot do that in isolation: we need to know the content of the discipline, and the sequence of that content, to shape our inquiries. Guidance on how to leverage your content to develop these subproblems, or investigations, occurs in the Module section in the next chapter; don't skip the Text Sets section on the way over there, either.

That said, one way you can get started even without knowing your texts or content is by thinking about the overarching problem and a sophisticated response as a set of components or parts. Earlier in the problem-formation process you thought through what such a response might entail—we can use that as a starting point to considering possible investigations, or the smaller problems that guide thinking toward the bigger problem. Some things you could consider include the following.

- The critical knowledge students would need to answer the overarching problem

- What the ambiguities, nuances, and shades of gray are in the problem or issue

○ What abstract concepts (for example, progress or justice) students should
define and wrestle with

○ What text or genre features students can analyze or apply to address
this problem

You can refine this initial list as you build the text set and then solidify it as you put
the module together.

As the steps suggest, the problem-formation process is marked by mindful trial and
error, making connections, generating ideas, and continual refining. In writing, it
may appear to be tedious and time consuming; in action, however, the thinking—or
dialogue with other teachers, if collaborating on the problem—usually takes only a
few minutes at a time. It is important, though, that there are multiple opportunities for these few-minute-long discussions. The problem is constantly reconsidered
and tweaked.

Finding Sources for Problem Formation

Still struggling with how to get started? Just look around you! Multiple sources are
present and ready to help: from societal concerns present and past; from our instruction materials, such as existing or developing syllabi, texts, essential questions, and so
on; and from our own lives and the lives of students—the problems of community,
school, and individual.

The World Around You

Intellectual and issue problems frequently come from the world at large—current
events, societal issues, and social and cultural matters that drive and define our
society. Notice the scope here: problems with this focus look beyond the immediate school or community environs and toward national and global matters, or to
humanity and humanist concerns. Such problems may derive from long-standing
issues (What counts as life? What caused the fall of the Roman Empire?), or they
may also arise from our everyday encounters with the world. On the summer day in
2015 when I write this sentence, *Go Set a Watchman* (Lee, 2015), a sequel of sorts,
has just been published. The book has readers puzzling over several emerging problems. Is Atticus Finch—the empathic and progressive hero of *To Kill a Mockingbird*
(Lee, 1960)—actually a racist (intellectual)? How does the book affect the legacy of
Harper Lee, its author (intellectual)?

The first flyby of Pluto also occurred on this day. Given what we have learned about
its size, shape, and relationship to one of its moons, Charon—which students can
learn about from reading articles and looking at the initial images and data—new

intellectual problems emerge. Is Pluto really a dwarf planet (intellectual)? Upon examination of the initial photos that have come in, what are the key geological features of the planet (interpretive)? In consideration of NASA's existing priorities, as well as new editorials on the subject, what should be the next priority for space exploration (issue)?

Instructional Materials

As rich and rigorous content, the best of your existing or potential content and complex texts articulate some of the key issues, problems, and interests of your discipline. They help dictate the kinds of problems your students will take up. Strong texts, ones with rich and complex language, also present challenges in determining the relationship between the meaning of the text and the use of language to express that meaning—the stuff of good interpretive problems.

Self and Students

You can draw problems from your own and your students' experiences, interests and wonderings, and challenges. Such problems may come from your own questioning of the discipline coursework and engagement with the world (see the previous section) or interactions within the school or community; you may put yourself in the shoes of your students and think about the questions they are likely to have (or should have!) about course content, their community, and their own existence. Student-generated problems themselves may also serve as a source for curricular focus.

Consider our ninth-grade example from earlier in the chapter: if the ultimate concern or interest of the school is improving student engagement and learning (goal), and if the instruction is to take place at the outset of the school year (context), then the problems guiding instruction, it follows, ought to not only reflect these matters but actually take them up. That is, the school is hoping a change to instructional programming results in positive changes to student thinking and behavior—so why not make this relationship and its potential outcomes a course of study? Going meta gives us two lines of inquiry already: (1) on a causal level, there's an opportunity to learn more about things like how schools work (or could work) and how people—adolescents, especially—think and act, and how various factors influence those concerns; (2) on an agentic and personal level, there's also an opportunity for individual students to reflect on their own thinking and behavior, propose changes to said thinking and behavior, make plans of action, and so on. That fits in perfectly with both the goals and time of year. Teachers in all content areas are initiating students into the norms and routines of their classrooms, so this could serve as a significant lever to both set classroom expectations and preview the kinds of literacy practices students will experience over the course of the year.

In concept and in language, what we want and ask students to know and do matters. That adage "task predicts performance" (City, Elmore, Fiarman, & Teitel, 2009, p. 30) rings true here. And now that we've talked about creating those problems, it's time to turn, in chapter 2, to solving them. The extent to which solving problems is at the center of classroom work, and the quality of said problems, is likely to predict the quality, rigor, and clarity of student engagement, performance, and achievement.

The Big Idea

Use the following key takeaways to review, reflect, and help introduce these concepts to others.

- The essence of ambitious instruction is solving meaningful, rigorous, discipline-specific problems by analyzing, evaluating, and developing new arguments from multiple texts—*synthesis*, in other words.

- Effective problems are topical and attentive to the core knowledge and ways of knowing of the content under study. They are relevant, argumentative, and sophisticated.

- To create good problems, teachers should look to both what is essential to know and do in their course and content area and what is meaningfully arguable within the content; in tandem with developing the problem, teachers should also articulate what a sophisticated response to the problem is.

Planning Ambitious Instruction: How to Connect Problems to Practice

Now that we have the foundation of high-quality problem formation in place, let's turn to creating a system and sequence of problem *solving*. Connecting the dots from problem to performance, this chapter continues to address the components of ambitious instruction by focusing on the following.

- **Performance assessments:** These are designed to answer a problem through synthesis.
- **Text sets:** These are groups of thematically linked texts that function as the content-area learning in support of the problem.
- **Modules:** These are road maps that guide learners from the launch to completion of the end assessment; the sequence of content and instruction designed to support preparation for answering the problem.

This chapter helps you put together a strong module for enacting ambitious instruction. By the time you're done reviewing and applying the concepts that follow, you'll have the tools in place to plan and enact your module on a daily basis (addressed in the subsequent chapters).

What follows is an evidence-based way of designing learning experiences. It is not—and should not be—the only way to do so. Absorb the following ideas; integrate them into your practice. But also feel free to be flexible and adaptive with them.

As noted, part of what makes ambitious instruction ambitious is its responsiveness to learners. The same flexibility should be available to teachers in planning.

Designing Performance Assessments

This one, at first glance, is fairly simple. Performance assessments ought to entail students answering or addressing your designated problem through and by using synthesis. That's it.

Okay, that's slightly complicated. But the principle is elemental. The problem *is* the assessment; a well-developed argument is the solution, from which you *gauge* performance. You know you have both assessment and performance when students can and must fully and independently respond to the problem in a multipage response that requires the use of multiple sources and in multiple modalities; that's a problem worth centering assessment *and* instruction around. You can add bells and whistles to the design—for example, a laboratory experiment, a debate, or a multimedia presentation—but some portion of every major assessment in your course of study should have some element of multisource argumentation to it. That's it.

This is not a new idea. It's not even a radical one anymore. Synthesis tasks now predominate most national-level, secondary-level curricula and assessments; it's the default assignment of most writing-intensive college courses. Figure 2.1 shares examples of the kind of performances grades 7 and 11 students are expected to enact on the ELA portions of major standardized assessments. Even if you are not an English teacher, pay close attention to the patterns at play. I'd also encourage you to review your local- and state-level assessments, if not one of the ones following, to see how they compare.

What did you notice? Both middle and high school standardized assessments ask your learners to draw from multiple sources to argue, analyze, and assess claims; in several cases, they even need to do so in time-limited settings. Some examples explicitly ask students to compare one source of content or ideas to others (for example, "Compare how . . ."); others lead with the task (for example, "Make a recommendation . . .") with the expectation of text usage. In all cases, they expect students to develop evidence-based claims that draw from what they have read and ask them to look beyond their reading by taking their own stances, articulating a shared or connecting idea, and so forth—synthesis, essentially.

None of the prompts included in figure 2.1 should look radically different from what you've seen or implemented yourself—that's the idea. Less immediately visible, though, is the fine print: the guidelines for these prompts convey the intellectual work behind the creation of the task; this is where we see the foundation for sophisticated thinking. Figure 2.2 (page 43) shows some of the response expectations for two of the grade 7 ELA prompts listed in figure 2.1.

	Assessments			
Curricula				
	EngageNY	Match	ACT	Smarter Balanced Assessment Consortium	Advanced Placement
Seventh Grade	You are part of the Children and Media Expert Advisory Committee. Your job is to help the American Academy of Pediatrics revisit the recommendation that children older than two should spend no more than two hours a day on entertainment screen time. After examining both the potential benefits and risks of entertainment screen time, particularly to the development of teenagers, make a recommendation. Should the AAP raise its recommended daily entertainment screen time from two hours to four hours? (7.4A.2, Lesson 17)	You have read two different texts about the American experience for Puerto Rican immigrants in the memoir *When I Was Puerto Rican* and in the song "America" from West Side Story. Compare how the author and song writer Esmeralda Santiago and Arthur Laurents convey the theme of the American Dream in each text. (7.102.27)	N/A	Using at least two sources, write an explanatory article about sleep and naps for the next issue of the school newspaper. The audience for your article will be other students, teachers, and parents. (Grade 7 Napping Explanatory Performance Task)	N/A

Source: ACT, n.d.; College Board, 2018; EngageNY, n.d.; Match Fishtank, n.d.a, n.d.b; SBAC, 2019a, 2019b.

continued ↓

Figure 2.1: Sample performance assessment prompts from national-level curricula and assessments.

	Curricula		Assessments		
	EngageNY	Match	ACT	Smarter Balanced Assessment Consortium	Advanced Placement
Eleventh Grade	Develop and present a claim about how Sherman Alexie's poem "How to Write the Great American Indian Novel" relates to central ideas or points of view developed in at least two of the four texts in this module. (11.2.2, Lesson 14)	Both Tennessee Williams and his character, Tom Wingfield, struggle to escape reality. Compare how each man struggles to escape reality by using details from both *The Glass Menagerie* and "The Catastrophe of Success." In your essay, be sure to reference specific literary or rhetorical devices used by the author to convey the struggle. (11.1.4)	Write a unified, coherent essay about the increasing presence of intelligent machines. In your essay, clearly state your own perspective on the issue and analyze the relationship between your perspective and at least one other perspective. (Writing Sample Essays, Essay Task)	Today, in preparation for the school board meeting, you will write a multiparagraph argumentative essay in which you take a stance on the topic of financial literacy courses. Make sure you establish an argumentative claim, address potential counterarguments, and support your claim from the sources you have read. (Grade 11 Mandatory Financial Literacy Argumentative Performance Task)	Carefully read the following six sources, including the introductory information for each source. Then synthesize material from at least three of the sources and incorporate it into a coherent, well-developed essay that defends, challenges, or qualifies the notion that eminent domain is productive and beneficial. (English Language and Composition, Section II, Question 1)

	EngageNY	SBAC
Sample Guidelines	• Present analyses and evaluations of two arguments related to the issue. • Establish the relevance of one argument's position and evidence to their own argument. • Respond to a divergent or opposing argument in an appropriate and strategic way. • Cite evidence from both texts to support their analyses and evaluations.	• Using more than one source, develop a thesis or controlling idea to explain about sleep and naps. • Select the most relevant information from more than one source to support your thesis or controlling idea. • Write a multiparagraph explanatory article explaining your thesis or controlling idea.

Source: EngageNY, n.d.; SBAC, 2019a.

Figure 2.2: Sample guidelines for grade 7 ELA performance assessments.

The guidelines in figure 2.2 note the kinds of evidence used, frequency of use, and analysis articulated, as well as how claims are to be generated and utilized—all the places in academic writing where rigor lives. Guidelines will vary by assessment and learning focus, of course, but the principle stays the same: we want students leveraging a multitude of ideas—analyzing them, applying them, assessing them—in service of developing their own perspectives. The idea here is simply to set up a task situation in which our learners must respond to the problem identified in a way that is commensurate with the richness of the prompt. So if the problem is *Is biology destiny?*, we might want students to construct a thesis built on the understanding and application of core course knowledge—such as the role genetics play in determining the behaviors and traits of offspring—to draw on multiple and varied examples, with specific interplay between in-class laboratory experiments and secondary sources (that is, not the textbook). We want students to read to address the problem and acknowledge the complexity of the issue by analyzing the strengths and weaknesses of counter or alternative perspectives. This helps clarify what a sophisticated response entails, and what we'll need to teach students to create such a response.

That's the big idea we're driving toward when thinking about the end assessment. Because the performance assessment conveys what students need to know and be able to do intellectually, instruction essentially exists to support them in developing and performing these intellectual behaviors. While the behaviors will change some depending on the kind of problem the students are solving and the form in which the response should take, there are some basic guidelines that every assessment should follow.

○ Students respond directly, formally, and individually to the overarching problem.

○ The task and response involve multiple standards, including at least one to two each that address argumentative writing, reading analytically with evidence, and researching or responding to multiple sources. (If you use the Common Core, for instance, good performance assessments will consistently address Writing anchor standards 1, 7, 8, and 9, and Reading anchor standards 3, 5, 7, and 8 [NGA & CCSSO, 2010].) Every time.

○ Students generate and test an original thesis, claim, or hypothesis.

○ The task and response require students to integrate at least three to four texts in their response, including the anchor text and a new text (see next section for more).

Simple, right? Naming what students should do is easy; the really hard part from a teacher-planning perspective is figuring out how to support them in accomplishing the essential parts of problem solving. We'll tackle the latter shortly; here, though, I want to wrap up the section with a surefire way to get your big-picture vision on paper and ready to go in roughly thirty to forty-five minutes once you have your problem articulated. I organize the five steps by component.

1. **Formalize the prompt:** You'll start here to answer or address your problem, and you'll draw on multiple sources to do so. If you're addressing an intellectual or issue problem, chances are you can take your problem and restate it as the prompt. Interpretive problems may require slight reworking to fit, such as specifying the texts or textual elements to be addressed (for example, *How do authors utilize symbols of light and dark to develop characters and comment on the story world?* may become *Compare the authors' use of light-dark symbolism in* _____ *[Text A] and* _____ *[Text B]*).

2. **Clarify the guidelines:** A synthesis task is going to require the use of many standards—after all, both reading and writing, if not additional speaking or multimedia demands, are going to be involved in responding to the problem—so what you ask students to do should both reflect grade-level expectations and draw explicitly from them. Use your state or national standards (or both) to select the learning benchmarks addressed or needed in order to fulfill the prompt. Use language drawn directly from them to populate your guidelines. If language in support of synthesis is missing from your standards, be sure to add those expectations. For example, you could add, "Develop an original, knowledgeable claim drawn from two or more texts you read in this module," "Provide evidence from at least three distinct sources," and the like.

3. **Expand the assessment parameters (as needed):** Here you can make additional decisions on the format, medium, component, audience, and so on beyond the basics of having students write an organized and formal academic response. For instance, you could ask students to submit a written paper to you but also present or debate their findings to the class; you might also specify who the audience is, the style or organization of the response, and so on. You'll want to reassess what to prioritize, too. Perhaps developing a multimedia or artistic representation of student understanding is the desired product, and thus the written response may require less formality, intensity, and time. Return to your guidelines and adjust accordingly.

4. **Ready the companion text:** Review the next section for guidance on selecting texts for instruction and assessment.

5. **Create the assessment tool:** Because the guidelines are based on the standards, and because the standards indicate what students should do to demonstrate rigor, you'll want to use the same language in your rubric or other assessment device. The key is to make clear how the assessment component is connected to the level of understanding or sophistication desired. That is, do not simply say "Uses two or more pieces of evidence from three sources" but instead "Uses specific, relevant evidence from two or more sources to convey the role genetic inheritance plays in survival." Note the inclusion of qualitative and quantitative components in the articulation of performance. Language is present to identify completion of the task components ("evidence from two or more sources"), the quality of work ("specific, relevant evidence"), and the desired demonstration of understanding expected of learners ("to convey"). You'll want to do so for all the assessment guidelines that you articulate. (Note: The learning trajectory activity described in chapter 5, page 159, may be of use in supporting, or even serving as, the assessment tool.)

Once you know where you're going, the next step is to determine the content, teaching, and additional instructional supports necessary to get (students) there.

Matching Content to Problems: Building an Effective Text Set

Problems are solved and synthesis is enabled by and through content, which you need to carefully select, sequence, and support for students to understand and own the intellectual labor in your classroom. That's content in plural form; synthesis, as noted elsewhere in the chapter, depends on integrating multiple ideas into a new or expanded vision, and that means multiple texts or voices. Variety is essential so that students can understand and engage in the complexity of, well, a complex topic.

The body of content that achieves this is called a *text set*. Essentially, text sets are selected literature drawn from different authors, reading levels, genres, and formats—including nonprint—that share a common concept or theme and can, in concert with one another, be used to address a problem and support inquiry. Though what might go into a text set will vary by discipline, all content areas can have text sets; in fact, disciplinarians in your field develop and use them all of the time. A historian, for instance, might analyze multiple primary sources from a certain era while using visual data and a secondary resource to understand the historical context surrounding said primary sources; a scientist might draw on results from previous studies and theoretical papers in academic journals to make sense of and assess her own data.

The same spirit of exploration inhabits the notion of organizing a set of content for your learners, only here you are carefully curating a set of sources on a given topic or problem to support and scaffold synthesis. Note the use of the word *curated*. You intentionally construct a text set for three purposes: to (1) help build the background knowledge necessary to understand key disciplinary content (comprehension), (2) provide a range of perspectives and ideas necessary for learners to analyze and assess the problem (critique), and (3) position students to answer, in writing or orally, the problem through the use of multiple sources of evidence.

Text sets are a relatively new concept in teaching, but initial research on their use suggests that reading multiple text types and perspectives on a shared topic is far more effective in supporting students' ability to identify and analyze relationships among ideas, issues, people, and so on than reading a single text on the same subject (James, Goldman, Ko, Greenleaf, & Brown, 2014; Litman et al., 2017; Young & Serafini, 2011). This is because text sets can be used to do the following.

○ Address the next generation learning standards' expectation that students read multiple texts on similar topics or themes in order to integrate knowledge and ideas (for example, CCRA.R.7–9) and write and research with multiple sources to build and present knowledge (for example, CCRA.W.7–9; NGA & CCSSO, 2010).

○ Increase the volume and range of students' reading, as well as build both general and disciplinary knowledge (Daniels & Zemelman, 2014; Lupo, Strong, Lewis, Walpole, & McKenna, 2018; Reisman, 2012).

○ Provide the background knowledge necessary to better understand complex texts *during* reading (Afflerbach & Cho, 2009; Arya, Hiebert, & Pearson, 2011).

- Increase the length and quality of students' written responses (Coombs & Bellingham, 2015).

- Build buy-in and understanding of the inquiry process (Ivey, 2002).

Text sets will vary in number and size based on the problem and amount of instructional time needed to solve it. Instructional goals are the priority, and they determine how students use the texts and how many of them there will be—not the other way around (Valencia et al., 2014). But you will want to consider several factors beyond instructional goals when selecting texts. These factors include the reading level of the texts and your students, the quality and sophistication of the arguments the texts make, and the diversity of ideas, voices, and perspectives presented in the texts.

Some have suggested that teachers select one extended, challenging text and surround it with two to three easier texts that can support background knowledge development (Lewis & Walpole, 2016; Lupo et al., 2018); others have argued for an approach in which six to eight short accessible texts supplement and support a long-form anchor text (Elish-Piper, Wold, & Schwingendorf, 2014). My personal preference is that students spend the most time possible with more challenging texts; a growing body of research supports this approach (Holmes, Day, Park, Bonn, & Roll, 2014; Kerlin, McDonald, & Kelly, 2010). Teachers would then compensate for the extra challenge with more intentional support and knowledge building (the theme of this book, essentially). Greater access to and more time with complex texts provides more practice in advance of learners' transition to the reading and writing they'll do in college or career. Provided there is adequate additional support, increased engagement with rich content will also provide the resources to read complex texts with greater independence when reading other texts in the set (Arya et al., 2011; Fisher & Frey, 2014; Williamson, 2008; Wixson & Valencia, 2014).

Types of Texts

My ideal text set is a purposeful mix of content learning that sets learners up to do rigorous work on their own. Each text has a purpose; each text is compatible with the others to enable and support synthesis. That's why I think of text sets less in terms of number of texts in a set and more in terms of type. What, in other words, will this text do to support my students' understanding and application? To help with that question, in the following sections, I describe several categories of texts that could populate your set purposefully and meaningfully. As you read through each, think about how this text type would aid your students' understanding of key concepts or problems in your coursework. Think, too, about what you already have or could use in existing or future text sets.

Launch Texts

You well know that the greater prior knowledge students have about the topics discussed in the texts, the easier it is for them to integrate the texts with one another or with other content (Bråten, Ferguson, Anmarkrud, & Stromso, 2013). Your starting text has to position students with the knowledge they need to engage subsequent texts. A launch text, then, is a short read designed to give students an initial and broad understanding of the problem—the landscape or "35,000-foot perspective" of the issue. This text should define issues and key terms or concepts and do so plainly and holistically. It should also serve as a hook, conveying the significance and relevance of the issue. For instance, if our problem is *Why is America so polarized, and what can we do about it?*, we might start first with the opinion essay "The Rich White Civil War" by *New York Times* columnist David Brooks (2018), which breaks down the root causes of the polarization and classifies the polarized into different categories. This organization provides students a foundation for the problem and a set of criteria and categories to apply to other content, such as data, excerpts from political science research, and differing perspectives from an array of stakeholders. You will typically choose one launch text.

Anchor Texts

These are the core texts of instruction, requiring the most instructional time and focus. Longer than the other texts, and with a level of linguistic and conceptual complexity at or above grade-level text complexity demands, these texts serve as the centerpieces for your inquiries. They should contain and propel the key ideas and arguments of the problem, such that students can connect what they have learned to the other texts in the set, and vice versa. In English, the anchor text is likely to be either a novel or book-length nonfiction work, an extended essay or literary text, or a set of short texts in the same genre (for example, a collection of poems). In social studies, longform primary sources (for example, the Constitution), historical analyses, or book-length secondary sources are your go-tos. For science, you're likely to consider journal articles, panel reports, and longer magazines reporting on scientific issues. For our *Why is America so polarized?* problem, a full-length social-historical analysis like *Bowling Alone* (Putnam, 2000) or a memoir like *Hillbilly Elegy* (Vance, 2016) are logical choices. Students can read most or all of an anchor text, or portions of several. You will typically choose one to two anchor texts.

Critical Perspectives

These texts serve the dual function of (1) providing different viewpoints on the issue to expand students' understanding of the problem and (2) serving as direction and evidence for crafting solutions to the problem. You can draw critical perspectives texts from essays or opinion articles, research or criticism, or biographical or personal writing. Comparing and contrasting approaches within the same genre—say, two different textbooks' interpretation of the same event—is also a possibility. We want texts that "talk" to one another. The stronger the relationship among texts, particularly if the relationship contains conflict, the more likely students are to use complex thinking to expand their understanding (Braasch & Bråten, 2017). The key is to strive for nuance and depth over simple dichotomies—that is, rather than simply look for and select dichotomous pro-or-con texts, which may give learners a superficial understanding of the extreme ends of opinion on the issue, we are looking for texts that will convey the complexity of the issue, such as the values in conflict, the possible solutions on offer, and the general "stickiness" of the issue. Thus, instead of finding two opposing sides, consider including two perspectives that offer the same or similar viewpoints but have different concerns or recommendations, or try to focus on different perspectives rather than merely different opinions—that is, the texts could share viewpoints but offer different solutions or recommendations. You might also choose different genres. Our social studies example, for instance, might draw on excerpts from books by politicians across the political spectrum, for example, Jeff Flake's (2017) *Conscience of a Conservative* and Elizabeth Warren's (2017) *This Fight Is Our Fight*. You will typically choose two to three critical perspective texts.

Lens Texts

Lens refers to a theoretical perspective, framework, or model that allows students to analyze and evaluate the claims and evidence of other texts in the set, which can then support students in creating their own arguments (Shanahan et al., 2016). Such texts can be as simple as a set of criteria for determining whether it is economically viable to use public dollars to pay for a new athletic stadium or as complex as an essay on feminist literary theory or a model of the space-time continuum. The length or text complexity matters less than the opportunity the text provides to students to interpret other texts—or the problem as a whole—critically. Given that you may draw the readings from research journals or other complex academic texts (that is, lengthy and verbose reads), a lens text probably shouldn't be more than a precise excerpt; a visual or informetric with some text may also suffice. (Note to middle school teachers: short excerpts from *The New York Times* or *Psychology Today* may be logical, grade-appropriate text-complexity sources in such cases.) In the case of our social studies example, we might choose an excerpt from "The Strengthening of Partisan Affect" (Iyengar & Krupenkin, 2018), a political science research article that introduces the concept of *negative partisanship*, which learners could use to guide their analyses of why the American electorate is so polarized. You will typically choose one to two lens texts.

Nonprint Sources

The definition of *texts* here includes all possible content students might interact with in service of achieving learning targets—think images, quantitative data, multimedia, and more. Nonprint sources have several instructional purposes, not the least of which is providing students with accessible visual representations of key concepts, which will further enable them to draw connections and synthesize across texts. Regularly including such texts also offers students more opportunities to realize grade-appropriate learning benchmarks, as the Common Core and most state standards all have standards calling for students to engage with nonprint sources. The selection of nonprint sources should be based on purpose: *What is it you want your students to understand about the content or the problem, and how can a nonprint representation help?* For our social studies example, for instance, if we want to provide additional perspectives on the issue, we might choose a political cartoon; if we want students to understand the scope or significance of the problem, we may choose survey data or a data table. You will typically choose one to two nonprint source texts.

Transdisciplinary Connections

Reading and applying a text from a different content area or a genre uncommon to the subject can help students draw connections and conclusions they wouldn't have made solely from reading within the content area. For instance, an English class may draw on a research study from the subfields of psychology to help with character analysis when reading a literary text. Science students might read a short literary text to understand the societal and ethical implications of scientific phenomena. What you want, in other words, is a text that will make your topic three-dimensional: it should add the human element that highly technical content (that is, science) may lack, and the science lens the humanities may need to be more than just theme and character. Thus, with our social studies example, students may benefit from reading sociology research on, say, one or more of those political tribes that have been influential in shaping the current political or cultural climate. An excerpt of a memoir from a member of one of those tribes—say, *Hillbilly Elegy* (Vance, 2016), mentioned earlier—may also suffice. You will typically choose one transdisciplinary connection text.

Performance Assessment Companion Text

The best way to encourage critical reading and synthesis on the performance assessment is to prompt students to integrate new ideas into their existing schemas, which they'll have developed during instruction leading up to the assessment. To do so, I recommend introducing one or two new texts of roughly two to four pages in total at the time of assigning and starting the performance assessment, with the expectation that students will incorporate the new text in the written response. Students will then read it independently—with the potential for some student-to-student engagement with it—during the week of the performance assessment. Purpose should dictate text selection; you want a selection that can expand or solidify students' emerging position and understanding. The text should not reiterate or summarize what students have already learned. Chances are you already have a good candidate from the texts you collected for the previous categories; if not, my preference here is usually an excerpt from one of the following: an additional lens text, a case study or example connected to or parallel to the problem, or a primary source document—such as voices from stakeholders in the problem, data connected to the problem, any policy documentation addressing the issue directly—that might offer additional nuances or perspective on the issue. Note the purposes here: students can use the lens text to analyze or assess a position. The examples or primary documentation can provide new evidence to expand or enhance a position. In the case of our social studies example, we might choose a sample case study or excerpt from *The Forgotten* (Bradlee, 2018), which chronicles the lives and reasoning of U.S. voters during the 2016 presidential election. You will typically choose one to two performance assessment companion texts.

Text Set Examples

I included examples of text sets from each content area in figure 2.3 (page 52). Note that the guiding problems, in bold, head each section of the figure. Notice the variety of text types, including visual texts, in the examples in figure 2.3. This variety is necessary in order to fully and meaningfully answer the guiding problem of the text set. The ideas the texts convey work together to ensure access to complexity, not simply to increase the difficulty of the reading. They also provide significant opportunities to support students in integrating multiple kinds of evidence into their speaking and writing. Notice, too, the frequent use of excerpted texts. Using short samples of sophisticated texts in turn increases access to the kinds of texts that can lead to or support more sophisticated responses—counterarguments, delineations or classifications of ideas, evaluations of underlying values, and so on. Finally, notice that there are no pro-and-con selections. This is because the problems demand definitions, solutions, and interpretations rather than simple yes-or-no stances. The text selections, in turn, must provide the content that can help students conceptualize the problem and possible solutions, not define it for them. The scope of the problem and the kinds of analysis and argument it demands shape the scope of the text set.

You'll also notice neither my descriptions nor the examples in figure 2.3 include textbooks. Few textbooks are written at the appropriate grade level, and few are likely to meaningfully address the problem you've designed. Their utility to inquiry-based learning is minimal. Textbooks discourage active engagement with the problem (Goldman et al., 2016). While there may be value in using textbooks as an additional source to build background knowledge, the readings that will best serve students' content and conceptual understanding and provide the volume and range needed to be able to read independently and for meaning in college and career come from and through the common genres of your discipline. Students will not be able to solve rigorous content-area problems without access to this kind of content.

English: What does it to mean to be an American?

Novel: *Americanah* (Adichie, 2013) or *The Great Gatsby* (Fitzgerald, 1925)

Poem: "Won't You Celebrate With Me" (Clifton, 2012)

Speech: Excerpts from inaugural addresses by Bill Clinton, George W. Bush, and Barack Obama

Essay: "What Does It Mean to Be an 'American'?" (Walzer, 1990)

Article: "American Dream, No Illusions; Immigrant Literature Now About More Than Fitting In" (Sachs, 2000)

Science: How should nation-states respond to the challenge of climate change?

Article: "The Physical Science Behind Climate Change" (Collins, Colman, Haywood, Manning, & Mote, 2007)

Data table: "Outlooks—Data Snapshots" (National Oceanic and Atmospheric Administration, n.d.)

Report: Excerpt from *Climate Change 2013: The Physical Science Basis* (Intergovernmental Panel on Climate Change [IPCC], 2014)

Report: Excerpts from World Bank's (2012) *Turn Down the Heat* series

Article: "A Grand Experiment to Rein in Climate Change" (Barringer, 2012)

Report: Excerpt from *Reframing the Problem of Climate Change* (Jaeger, Hasselmann, Leipold, Mangalagiu, & Tabara, 2012)

Social studies: What is the true legacy of the Great Migration?

Nonfiction book: Excerpts from *The Warmth of Other Suns* (Wilkerson, 2010)

Primary source: "South Unable to Put Stop to Negro Exodus" (*Washington Times*, 1916; newspaper article)

Historical analysis: Excerpt from *The Southern Diaspora* (Gregory, 2005)

Paintings: Jacob Lawrence's *Migration Series* (1940–1941; Turner, 1993)

Fiction: Excerpt from *The Twelve Tribes of Hattie* (Mathis, 2013)

Figure 2.3: Sample content-area text sets.

Curating Text Sets

The key to building an effective text set is ensuring both alignment and accessibility: *alignment* in terms of linking texts so they are relevant to the problem which they support and will position students to solve, and *accessibility* in terms of including texts of varying types and at varying levels of difficulty to ensure all students have opportunities to engage the content successfully (Elish-Piper et al., 2014). Given its close alignment to the problem that students are solving and its role in creating access points to solve it, a text set isn't just a compendium of content; it's a sequence and scaffold for how students will engage in inquiry. The following list summarizes the key features of text sets.

- Directly and cumulatively address the problem.

- Draw from multiple genres, mediums, and text types.

- Provide a range of perspectives and insights on the problem.

- Appear in an order that increases students' sophistication of understanding of the topic or problem.

- Support writing from and with multiple sources.

To meet these criteria, you'll want to take an intentional approach to building out your content selections. Here's one process to do so.

1. **Unpack the problem:** As we saw in the performance assessment section, the first step is to make sure you understand what a sophisticated response is to the problem you've developed, both in terms of the conceptual understanding and the skills or performances demonstrated. If you haven't done so already, think carefully about the best answer to the problem: *What knowledge, know-how, and evidence would someone need in order to fully address the problem and be up to standard in a written response?* If you can identify these, you can identify texts that best address them.

2. **Select the anchor text:** Because the anchor text will be the one on which you spend the most time—either because it is book-length or because students read it multiple times—you'll want to select this text first. You likely have an anchor text in place or in mind; if you don't, or are seeking a new one, I would select one based on the following four criteria.

   a. Addresses many or all the criteria you identified in the previous step

   b. Demands to be read closely in order to be understood and analyzed

   c. Has a level of intellectual richness that warrants significant instructional time

   d. Can connect to or be supported by surrounding supplemental texts

   In short: this text should be complex in both language and knowledge demands and consistent with instructional goals.

3. **Identify critical perspectives:** Start by identifying the multiple perspectives on the problem, pushing yourself to think beyond simple pro-or-con perspectives—they rarely help students fully understand the issue, in large part because much of what is available for classroom use is extraordinarily dumbed down. Ask yourself, "Does this text give new

information or insight that will help students answer the problem with rigor and sophistication?" Look for texts that have nuance and perspective. Maybe they propose a surprising solution or provide more insight into the complications of existing solutions. Maybe it's a poem or results from a laboratory study that challenge or contrast with the anchor text. Indeed, don't feel like you have to limit yourself to argumentative writing, either. Personal accounts or essays, research, and even literary or imaginary accounts could work. But here, too, you'll want to ensure that the text and excerpts you use are at or above the grade-level-appropriate text complexity markers.

If you're struggling to locate appropriate texts here, one approach I find useful is to ask yourself, "What would a _____ (for example, sociologist, person living at the time) write about the problem or issue?" Go through various perspectives and consider what sort of genres or formats they'd look for or develop, and use those ideas to guide your search and selection.

4. **Complete the set by focusing on range:** Here you'll fill in the remaining pieces of your text set puzzle, looking for opportunities to integrate new genres, perspectives, and hooks.

   a. *Nonprint*—An easy starting point is to consider whether the problem is closer on the spectrum to social or scientific issues or to aesthetic or philosophical issues. If the former, quantitative data are likely to be your best bet; reports from governmental organizations or nonprofits are good sources. If the latter, you'll likely want visual representations—images, multimedia, and so on.

   b. *Transdisciplinary*—Use the perspective-taking approach described in the previous step to assist.

   c. *Performance assessment companion text*—As I said earlier in the section, the ideal text will be a two- to four-page piece or excerpt that either helps students to refine and enhance their claims or provides new evidence that can challenge or support their reasoning. Check what you've reviewed already for the other categories to see if any text (or portion of it) applies to these criteria; if none do, I recommend a text that introduces a complementary theory or concept, and for the latter, either new data, case studies, or explanations of real-life examples connected to the problem, or personal accounts that challenge students' initial beliefs.

   d. *Launch text*—I recommend doing this one last—knowing with what else students will engage will better help you ascertain where to begin. In this instance, you're looking for a text that is accessible, provides enough context and background knowledge to launch learners into the problem-solving process, and sets up engagement in the other texts. That's no easy feat. Newspaper and magazine journalism are particularly good for this selection because of their accessible organization, style, and ideas; the context necessary to understand the content is contained within the text.

After carefully reading this list, you can use the simple template in figure 2.4 (page 56) to help you take notes on potential additions to your text set.

You may need to repeat steps if the selection of one text demands or inspires a change to another. Iteration is the idea, and if you're inspired by these ideas, chances are you're going to have a clearer idea of how to engage your students in them.

Once you've got a good working draft, your last step before formalizing an instructional plan (see the next section) will be putting the texts in an initial order that can guide said planning. You already know that the launch text is going to appear first, and the performance assessment companion text is at the end—but how do you utilize and sequence texts between? To determine that order, you'll want to consider the following four criteria.

1. **Text complexity:** It may help to sequence texts by difficulty, with texts that are shorter or those with less discipline-specific vocabulary placed first to prepare students for comprehension of later texts that may be longer and more conceptual or syntactically challenging.

2. **Task complexity:** What you ask students to do with the texts should be both responsive to the complexity of the text and build toward engaging with more complex texts. For instance, you may want to position activities so that students first get opportunities to compare the claims and evidence of two or more texts before using the lens or nonprint texts in the set to evaluate or create arguments in response to reading; you may also want to wait until later in the text set to do more guided inquiry, where students help shape the process. (See chapter 3, page 69.)

3. **Synthesis potential:** To encourage hypothesis or claim making and novel thinking, you'll also want to deliberately sequence texts to give students opportunities to have their emerging understanding and arguments challenged and extended. Look for opportunities to pair or connect texts that present conflicting information, or to juxtapose texts that may illuminate ideas about the problem that would otherwise not surface without the texts speaking to one another.

Unpack the problem

What knowledge, know-how, and evidence would someone need in order to fully address the problem and be up to standard in a written response?

Select the anchor text: _____

Identify critical perspectives

Complete the set by focusing on range

Nonprint

Transdisciplinary

Performance assessment companion text

Launch text

Figure 2.4: Text set builder template.

*Visit **go.SolutionTree.com/instruction** for a free reproducible version of this figure.*

4. **Problem potential:** Be sure to intentionally sequence texts to build students' ability to answer the overarching problem that the text set addresses. In other words, the order of texts should help develop and accumulate students' understanding of, claims for, and evidence in support of solving the problem (Goldman et al., 2016).

Unless you have some investigations in mind already, you may not know what your tasks will be just yet; however, playing with these criteria can assist in forming the task. I'd suggest starting by laying out an order and interaction of texts you think will best set students up to answer the problem (problem potential). I would then look to add or enhance opportunities for students to juxtapose different texts in the text set (synthesis potential), which will likely occur between halfway and three-quarters of the way into the sequence of texts. Tweak the initial order so that it responds to the demands of the texts, making sure background knowledge demands and length or language complexities are supported appropriately (text complexity). This should then give you clarity on how to attend to the role of the task in response to and in support of the texts (task complexity).

Almost there!

Scoping and Sequencing Modules: A Cure for the Common Unit Plan

I'm not inherently opposed to unit plans. While the title of this section may suggest otherwise, there are times—say, a novel study in an English course or an extensive laboratory experiment in a science class—when a four- to six-week block of instruction is warranted, even necessary. But, for the most part, length shouldn't be the deciding factor in determining what to teach or the intensity with which to teach it. Our attention must remain on ensuring that what we ask students to do supports their intellectual development, and that our instructional support provides what students require to develop intellectually.

The big idea in the paragraphs ahead is that finding balance between time and focus requires an intentionality to planning that we often miss as we understandably try to pull together and plan a full year of instruction. Teachers plan and enact units not because there is any evidence base in support of them but because that's what they've always done. Tradition, not transformation, dictates their actions. Think about it: have your most valuable learning experiences, whether as teacher or learner, ever been because of a lengthy and linear survey of some topic or theme? I'd argue not. The best, most natural learning is usually in sustained, shorter bursts, with real and varied opportunities to plan, test, and question the acquired knowledge and skills; then we do it all over again. Again and again.

Our instructional plans should reflect that. Essentially, we want to tie assessment and instruction more closely. If we see the two as one, and build in the time to make them one, we can better support students in doing complex intellectual work. Put another way: when learning, doing, and performing are intertwined and constant, the amount of instructional time devoted to the work is not arbitrary (that is, four-to six-week chunks); rather, it is calibrated to the task. There will be task situations where we are concentrating on a specific set of knowledge or skills or performances that require focused attention, which may only need a finite and bounded set of instructional time to complete. There will be other situations—as I noted in the previous paragraph—that require more expansive uses of time. Three days, one week, two weeks—the problems we ask students to solve, and the process by which we problem solve, dictate length.

Thinking in Terms of Modules

Because this sort of thinking about instructional plans depends on the idea of flexible and flexibly long blocks of instruction, I refer to said blocks as *modules*. I'm not the first: the EngageNY (n.d.) curriculum, for instance, uses the same term to connote the blocks of instruction that comprise its yearlong scope and sequences. In that curriculum, the modules tend to be much longer, often comprising multiple units, but the principle is similar: instruction is built around summative performance assessments—called end-of-module assessments—with units of varying length, some no longer than three to five lessons, structured and sequenced to build students toward that performance assessment.

Think of modules, then, as simply blocks of instruction that include the time, activity, support, and assessments necessary to build toward a more meaningful, more rigorous culminating task (that is, a performance assessment) in the future. Modules form mini-units with their own activities and assessments (called *investigations*), but they also are connected with other modules to form longer sets of learning, helping students integrate understanding across texts and tasks. On average, they are several days of instruction—enough time, essentially, to inquire into content-area problems, read part or the whole of multiple complex texts, conduct short research or analytical writing, and so on.

Let's run with this idea of modules as units within units, with standards and texts aligned across modules to support student growth in the core content and the skills being assessed. You can, in other words, keep the topical or thematic units that are already in your curriculum. The change comes in the deliberate sequencing and scaffolding around problems big and small(er), complemented by texts and tasks high in rigor. Notice how in figure 2.5 (pages 59–60) a unit on climate change is positioned to help grades 11–12 students learn in intellectually significant ways, from reading about science issues, to doing science, to taking stances on a science issue. Students experience a range of texts and tasks on the way to constructing their own texts in response. This unit features both a pre- and post-assessment to measure content knowledge and skill transfer. In between, it includes work around a small set

Problem: What policy recommendations on climate change would you make to the next president?

	Assessed Standards	Texts	Problem Guiding Investigation	Analytical Writing Task
Formative Preassessment	CCRA.W.1, CCRA.W.9, RST.11–12.2, RST.11–12.3, RST.11–12.8	"The Other Inconvenient Truth" plus mock directions for a lab experiment (Foley, 2010)	N/A (selected- and short constructed-response test)	
Module 1	RST.11–12.7, RST.11–12.2, W.11–12.2	"The Physical Science Behind Climate Change" (Collins et al., 2007); data from the National Oceanic and Atmospheric Administration (n.d.); excerpts from *Climate Change 2013: The Physical Science Basis* (IPCC, 2014)	What are the measures for studying climate change, and what change has been measured? How do we know what causes change?	Summary of current data and consensus on climate science
	RST.11–12.8, RST.11–12.9, W.11–12.2	Excerpts from *Global Warming of 1.5 °C* (IPCC, 2018); "Increases in Global Temperature: What It Does and Does Not Tell Us" (Marshall, 2003)	What are we talking about when we talk about climate change?	

Source for standards: NGA & CCSSO, 2010.

Figure 2.5: Sample set of modules for a high school earth science course.

continued ↓

Module 2	RST.11–12.3, RST.11–12.9, W.11–12.7	Laboratory instructions	How do we measure the composition of the atmosphere, and what do those measurements mean?	Laboratory exercise: measuring carbon dioxide plus a short lab report comparing how findings compare to those in Module 1 reports
Module 3	RST.11–12.2, RST.11–12.8, W.11–12.8	*Turn Down the Heat* (World Bank, 2012); "A Grand Experiment to Rein in Climate Change" (Barringer, 2012); *Reframing the Problem of Climate Change* (Jaeger et al., 2012)	What are the near- and long-term consequences of climate change? What appears to be the most logical or most effective response?	Evaluation of solutions and recommendations
Summative Performance Assessment	CCRA.W.1, CCRA.W.8, RST.11–12.7, RST.11–12.9, CCRA.W.4–6	Unit texts plus outside research	What policy recommendations on climate change would you make to the next president?	A formal, researched essay or report

of standards within each module and increasingly more challenging work with the same standards across the modules. A series of interrelated and authentic intellectual problems on the topic or issue guides the work, using a set of analytical writing tasks developed in class. The instruction culminates in a formal writing assignment that serves as the summative performance assessment.

The key here, regardless of the duration of each component, is synergy. Daily instruction builds on a conceptual skill, practice tasks help integrate these skills, and the culminating performance assessment—as we learned in the previous section—has students demonstrate that integration in multiple ways and mediums. As the example in figure 2.5 illustrates, you can organize and bookend several modules with pre- and post-assessments to form a unit or quarter of instruction, with the modules functioning as a set of ongoing steps and benchmarks leading up to a final performance. You can also have modules contribute to the ongoing completion of that end result. For example, if the goal is to have students compose an argument on a content-area problem, one approach is to give them practice in smaller chunks within each investigation prior to assigning an essay or in-class writing prompt. Alternatively, the modules might serve to address individual components of the culminating performance assessment by helping students conduct research or develop a claim for the essay, for example. You can arrange these modules so that what you ask students to read and do grows increasingly more rigorous, leading up to an extended and independent performance assessment through writing or speaking. The performance assessment itself can be a module with research minilessons and elements of the writing process (such as brainstorming, drafting, and presenting) spread over the course of several days or weeks of preparation, composition, and publication of the assessment task.

Designing Modules: Your Turn

In its simplest form, a module buildout is just the alignment of your content (texts), focus (problems), and learning goals (standards) with the culminating performance assessment in an order that benefits learners' ability to perform up to standard on the latter. But this is teaching: it's complex and not without reason if our goal is to improve academic and instructional rigor. In that sense, what we want modules to be, essentially, is the intentional chunking of instruction into multiday investigations to provide learning experiences in which students:

- Have multiple exposures to and opportunities to practice with complex texts

- Respond to and solve authentic and meaningful problems of the given content area

- Receive guided support on how to analyze these texts

○ Collaborate with peers on developing conceptual understanding on content from complex texts

○ Demonstrate this emerging conceptual writing in speaking and writing

○ Develop and support their ability to demonstrate proficiency on an ongoing or subsequent performance assessment

Let's take the simple and complex mindset and apply it to creating a module. If you've reviewed and tried out the guidance in the previous sections, you've already got most of the raw materials you need: your problem, your end-of-module performance assessment and the standards it addresses, your texts, maybe even some subproblems. (If you haven't, you might want to double back and get caught up.) Look at the blank module template in figure 2.6. See how you can start filling in the top (problem) and bottom (performance assessment)? We know where we are going—let's now figure out how to get there.

Problem:			
Assessed Standards	**Texts**	**Problem Guiding Investigation**	**Analytical Writing Task**
Module 1			
Module 2			
Module 3			
Summative Performance Assessment			

Figure 2.6: Module builder template.

*Visit **go.SolutionTree.com/instruction** for a free reproducible version of this figure.*

Recognizing that sequence—especially of the texts—is important (Lupo, McKenna, & Walpole, 2015). We want the order of teaching and learning to:

- Address the standards or expectations of the performance assessment throughout the module

- Provide repeated or extended exposure both to the anchor text and to comparing texts in the text set

- Give students exposure to the process and content of engaging in inquiry around the issue or problem

- Prepare students, through formative tasks, to demonstrate understanding of the concepts, skills, or performances of the culminating assessment

We can begin to tease that sequence out by returning to this running theme of a sophisticated response—that is, what we identified in an earlier section as what an informed, up-to-standard performance on the culminating assessment entails in terms of the content and conceptual knowledge that it conveys, the analytical reading and writing comprehension it demonstrates, and so forth. To begin to break this down, it helps to think of it through the lens of the texts you selected for your text set: that is, What would students need to understand about these texts—whether individually or in tandem—in order to apply and integrate them when responding to the performance assessment? Because the answers to this question get at the essential understandings of the planned instruction, you can, in turn, use them to formulate investigations for a specific module. For instance, with the example in figure 2.5 (page 59), imagine we identify that students should see the immediate effects of climate change as the greater frequency of severe weather and be able to articulate some longer-term effects of dramatic changes to climate and ecosystems. We know, then, that we want students to define and delineate the impact of climate change (for example, *What are the near- and long-term consequences of climate change?*), and we also know that we want to build students up to make policy recommendations, hence the need to leverage the named effects in service of assessing solutions (for example, *What appears to be the most logical or most effective response?*). Note how we connect everything at once here, considering the overarching problem, the performance assessment, and the texts together to help us to begin to devise the component chunks that will comprise our instructional path.

Your turn. With an overarching problem, assessment, and text set you're working on, see if you can generate, say, two to four subproblems from connecting these pieces, putting them in an initial order that makes sense given the texts and the end assessment. This may change. If you're struggling to generate these subproblems, another way to come up with them is through the problem types discussed earlier in the chapter. Identify the issue, intellectual, or interpretive problems presented in your texts or the overarching problem, and select the problems that best tie back to the content and assessment.

Next, we can use the initial investigations you've developed to do two things: (1) identify the texts that best address them and (2) develop an interim writing task for the specific module that can serve the dual role of setting students up for the performance assessment and providing you with ways of monitoring and supporting student progress. The former is relatively self-evident—you already connected investigations to the texts in the previous step—but for the latter you'll want to review the standards being assessed by your performance assessment against the investigation and texts you've assigned to a given module: that is, What knowledge, skills, and performances in the standards pair best with the investigation and texts? In the second module of our example, for instance, we know from our investigation that our goal is to understand how to measure changes to the atmosphere; we also know from our standards—in this case, the Common Core—that one of the standards of the performance assessment, RST.11–12.9, calls on students to, "Synthesize information from a range of sources (e.g., texts, experiments, simulations) into a coherent understanding of a process, phenomenon, or concept, resolving conflicting information when possible" (NGA & CCSSO, 2010). Using language from the standard in conjunction with the goal of having students understand a scientific process, we reach the logical conclusion: students would best learn by doing, trying out the process of taking measurements they're studying, and comparing them to findings from other sources (such as from module 1). Thus, students should conduct a short lab experiment and write-up, and the core text would be the lab instructions or model.

There really are no tricks to what I did to create the plans in figure 2.5 (page 59). I knew where I wanted students to go, so I aligned each module to the goal to ensure students were getting meaningful doses of the content, skills, and performances necessary to get there. Once you know the investigation you're trying to solve and the texts to support it, what you're really doing is taking the core practice of the given standards and using them to determine what students will be doing to answer the investigation—for example, a summary, a lab report, parts of the performance assessment, and so on. From there you can build out the set of task components that lead to it. That's it.

As you continue to align texts and tasks, you should expect that some tweaking will be necessary to ensure the best fit; it will not be perfect at first. Here are some pointers to assist with the buildout.

- Treat the performance assessment as its own module, organizing three to seven days, depending on the demands of the task, for teaching or reteaching of core concepts and skills, independent work time on the task, and performance or sharing.

- A good starting point for sequencing the modules is to put the ones with the most accessible investigations and texts at the outset and the more challenging closer to the end. Notice how in figure 2.5 (page 59) we slot our launch text ("The Other Inconvenient Truth" [Foley, 2010]) and lab directions first, as they are in a familiar style and require or demand the least amount of background knowledge on the problem; the interim task is a summary, less demanding intellectually than the subsequent lab report and evaluation task. Later, students will engage reports or white papers from scientists and more complex data, which they will better be able to navigate after the initial orientation to the topic and scientific practices.

- I would engage the anchor texts somewhere between a third to halfway through the learning sequence. This will allow for the appropriate amount of instructional time to address it in full (if an extended text) or to reread it alongside other texts in the set (if a shorter text).

- A preassessment to launch the first module is not necessary but can be of great help if you're trying to pinpoint where students are and where they might have challenges with the conceptual or performative aspects of the culminating assessment. This can be as formal as having students write a mini-essay on the overarching problem or as informal as small groups of students discussing their initial perceptions of the problem. The purpose is to collect data on what students know and will need to know or be able to do to respond fully and meaningfully at the end of the module.

Iterate is a groan-inducing word, but you'll find it should feel natural and efficient to move module parts around, not to mention potentially tweak the other components as you clarify the best fit. And it won't take any longer than it normally would to sequence a unit, promise.

Putting the Pieces Together

To acknowledge the obvious: that was a lot.

So, rather than summarize or try to reduce, here's a shorter and simpler solution: find your entry point. Start with something small and accessible in your existing curriculum—say, one unit—rather than trying to do the entirety of your scope and sequence in one fell swoop. You don't necessarily have to start over; in fact, the easiest entry point is to pick an opportunity where a few of the pieces are already in place but would benefit from a more coherent supporting cast. Perhaps you already have a good problem or text set in place but what you are asking students to do with it on the culminating or interim assessments are not commensurate with your vision. Perhaps the assessment is in place but the content or learning sequence leading up to it does not put students on a pathway to get there. What is that one way or space where you can get started and where starting would provide immediate benefits to your planning? (Of course, if you're ready to go and have the space or need to revamp an existing chunk or all of your instruction, great!)

But let's say you're really struggling with an entry point: either the pieces, the process, or both are overwhelming and complicated. What now?

One option is to gather like-minded or role-alike peers and try to problem solve in the areas of weakness or need you or others have. For instance, you could discuss some of the critical problems, past and present, of your discipline. What, in other words, are disciplinarians (for example, historians, scientists, writers, critics, and so on) trying to know or solve? Next, examine your existing materials and resources—your texts, your curriculum, and so forth—and discuss what you have and need. What critical problems of your content area are you addressing already, and what problems are lacking or could be addressed inside existing or potential units of instruction? From here, you can start the development process by engaging any or all of the following.

- Study or compare unit or lesson plans in existing curricula to brainstorm potential problems.

- Read existing or potential texts in your curriculum, and generate ideas for problems connected to or arising from the texts.

- Consult exemplars, such as assessment constructs (for example, AP, PARCC, or SBAC) or high-quality curricular resources (for example, Stanford History Education Group's Reading Like a Historian plans; https://sheg.stanford.edu/history-lessons).

But a team or crowdsourcing approach may not be an option or even an asset when you start; you may need to go at this alone. For that, and for when you're not sure how to start, I'm actually going to suggest what might at first appear to be a counterintuitive idea: start with the text set. I know what you're thinking; doesn't the text set require knowing what the problem is, and isn't it a rather time consuming first step when the other pieces aren't in place yet? Sure, you'll need to have at least an initial impression of the problem space—knowing the general topic or issue should suffice—but I find the initial reading and exploration can be of significant help when trying to refine your problem and define the essential understanding and skills for students to learn. Refer back to figure 2.4 (page 56) to help organize your thoughts as you build a text set, and then use figure 2.7 to guide you through thinking not only about the problem but also about the assessment and the sequence of learning that may occur to lead up to it.

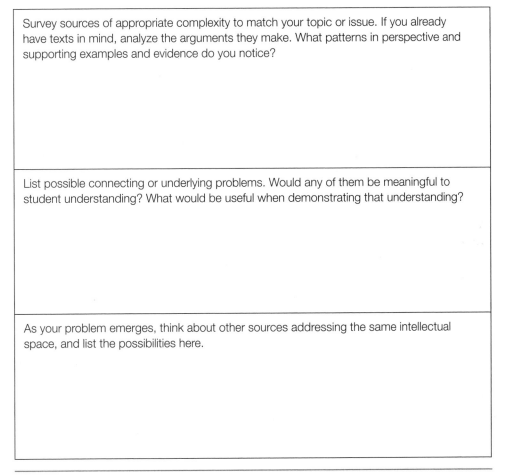

Figure 2.7: Using a text set to generate a problem.

*Visit **go.SolutionTree.com/instruction** for a free reproducible version of this figure.*

The Big Idea

Would it surprise you to know that regular engagement in analysis and argument from multiple sources during classroom instruction remains quite rare in secondary classrooms (Litman et al., 2017)? Probably not. Designing and facilitating problem-based and synthesis-focused learning is tough work; it may also be a lot of work at the outset. But the main problem isn't so much time or schedules or selecting the perfect content; it is problems themselves. What we ask students to do rarely consists of or demands engagement with multiple sources. If we want to change that, we will have to shift our perspectives from seeing our roles as simply teachers of content or texts to seeing texts as the means to help students solve the kind of problems that require text sets to solve. Texts are important; they are also inextricably linked to problems and tasks. They are the conversation and evidence, but it is what we ask students to do—the task—and what instructional supports we provide that drive student engagement. We'll cover tasks in the next chapter.

The big takeaways from this chapter for your review and reflection include the following.

- Instruction should culminate in students directly responding to the guiding problem, utilizing evidence from multiple sources to construct their arguments.

- Students need to purposefully and repeatedly engage with multiple forms of texts. These multiple texts are together known as a text set.

- Students need lengthy experiences with multiple dimensions of a problem, including through multiple texts and in varying task situations; this is the modular approach.

- The unifying device and initiator for planning ambitious instruction is understanding and articulating what a sophisticated student response would be to the overarching problem. Knowing what intellectual work looks like in response to the problem allows teachers to select and sequence content and instruction to support it.

Implementing Ambitious Instruction

Picture a typical high school U.S. history class in the spring: the sprint is on to reach contemporary times and wrap up, well, America in a pretty bow. Imagine the classroom nearing the end of a module examining the Cold War, with the teacher asking students to address the following guiding question: *How should history view the Soviet Union?* Two political cartoons and an excerpt from a book on the fall of the Soviet Union are the content for this single lesson.

Great problem, right? Sure, you could quibble with the wording, but how could you not love a task situation that positions students as historians, engaging them not only in a relevant problem of the discipline but also with some of the tools of the trade to answer it? You're probably already envisioning how you would facilitate it yourself.

The teacher provides a worksheet with questions for each source, assigning students to read each source individually and then answer the questions on the corresponding worksheet. Students did not receive instructions or structures for completing the activity; the teacher neither encouraged nor discouraged collaboration. As the students work on the assignment—some alone, some with elbow partners—the teacher walks around the room, helping students when their comprehension breaks down. At the end of the period, with about three minutes to spare, he has students answer the guiding question via an exit ticket.

You can guess what the student work looked like: brief, basic, lacking. Though the teacher could very clearly articulate to me afterward the level of sophistication he was looking for in students' thinking, without supports—the structures for inquiry, collaboration, and expression necessary to help students engage in rigorous tasks—there was simply no way for him or his students to realize sophisticated thinking. Without capital-T teaching his learners how to engage meaningfully and rigorously with the task and content he constructed, students were at a loss, struggling without purpose and conveying, at best, surface-level understanding. Product, sadly, equaled process.

To state the obvious: problem-based learning is only as effective as the support that students receive to do the work—that is, we must teach them the knowledge, skills, and dispositions to engage in it (Fisher, Frey, & Hattie, 2016). A good task, as you'll learn in this chapter, is not enough: it must be matched with and supported by an equally rigorous way of achieving it. That means making deliberate decisions about how to set up and launch a task, structure and sequence inquiry, and position students to learn from one another. It also requires responsive facilitation in the moment, both to anticipate potential struggles and opportunities and to use feedback to drive and sustain student engagement during ambitious intellectual work (Coombs & Bellingham, 2015). The big, big idea: teaching inquiry is realized in action, not planning.

Implementing Ambitious Instruction: The Fundamentals

The previous chapters laid out the *what* of ambitious instruction: your curriculum should be entirely focused on supporting students' ability to answer rigorous and relevant problems of your discipline. Now let's tackle the *how*—that is, the structure and sequence necessary to make it happen every day.

To do so, I've broken down the foundations of implementing ambitious instruction into five components: (1) *task potential*, or what comprises a task that can support and sustain student inquiry; (2) *task access*, or how all students receive entry points to do the work of the task; (3) *inquiry space*, or how to organize inquiry to structure or guide students' access to content; (4) *interactive argumentation*, or how to set students up to collectively engage in claim making or hypothesis testing; and (5) *multitext integration*, or how students make sense of and leverage multiple sources in support of inquiry. While I explain each individually in the pages that follow, you'll see in figure 3.1 that they are deeply intertwined; they depend on one another. The Organizing Ambitious Instruction section of the chapter (page 83) integrates them into a learning model and sequence, hereafter called an *investigation*.

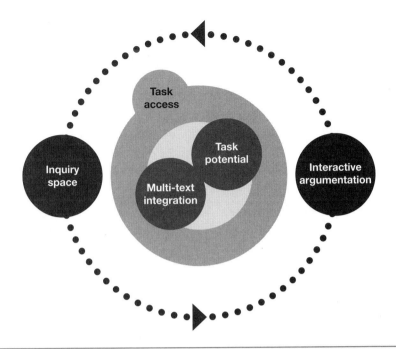

Figure 3.1: Five components of implementing ambitious instruction.

Task Potential

Common parlance denotes the word *task* as anything we ask students to do in a formalized academic setting: a group activity, homework, paper—are all considered tasks. This doesn't feel particularly helpful. It conflates tasks with words like *activity*, *assignment*, and so on. It doesn't distinguish for teachers and leaders what it would mean to focus improvement efforts on tasks.

I see it differently. *Task*, as used in this book, refers to everything that students do in service of answering the problem guiding the investigation (for each module) or performance assessment (in the module for the performance assessment). Essentially, it *is* the investigation—the content, instruction, activities, and assessment that get the students going on doing problem-based learning. A great task, then, is more than a prompt that has a high level in Webb's (1997) DOK or Bloom's (1956) taxonomy. It is the work and activity and teaching that engage students in core concepts and processes of your respective subject areas—developing hypotheses on scientific phenomena, analyzing primary and secondary sources surrounding a historical event, taking critical stances on literature, and so on—in service of solving the core problems of your discipline.

The distinction isn't just semantics. First, if we're going to make good on enacting problem- and inquiry-centered teaching and learning, what we ask students to do has to be in service of their learning—in this case, answering a relevant and rigorous subject-area concern. The problem is essentially the task; the investigation—if not the module itself—supports it. Second, reframing tasks this way shifts the primary driver of task design and implementation from time to inquiry. When tasks are simply what the teacher assigns students to do, they are shaped more so by limitation than possibility—for example, how many minutes are in the period or block. When we prioritize the problem-solving process, we shift the focus away from trying to fit activities or assignments into single lessons or even weeks and instead think holistically about all the components necessary for students to solve the problem with proficiency. We call this *task potential.*

Task potential encompasses the elements for students to potentially have a meaningful learning experience: the problem, the process, the product, and the performance criteria. Elements that define task potential are those that prompt and enable students to (Boston, 2012):

- Solve directly a meaningful and rigorous problem or guiding question

- Engage in complex, multistep reading, writing, and thinking processes

- Elaborate on arguments and reasoning; integrate evidence from texts into these stances

- Analyze patterns or trends; draw conclusions and claims based on these patterns, and articulate through writing and speaking

- Follow or leverage a prescribed or previously learned procedure

As noted throughout this book, it is necessary to adopt this inclusive and comprehensive view of facilitating student learning because administering a task with high cognitive demand, while critical, is alone not sufficient to enable and ensure rigor; in fact, research has shown that even with a promising task most teaching is implemented in ways that diminish the intellectual integrity of what students are being asked to do (Hiebert et al., 2003). Teachers, then, must be able to *maintain* and support cognitive complexity throughout implementation.

One way to think about task potential as a kind of momentum *across* instruction is to return to the concept of synthesis that we unpacked in chapter 1 in figure 1.2 (page 27). We can structure and scaffold instructional time devoted to engaging in complex, multistep processes (Boston, 2012) so that over the course of a module and investigation we ask students to do increasingly more rigorous problem solving. They can move from concrete activities—such as summarizing or identifying evidence—to those that are more abstract, like applying or creating theories to developing solutions. Doing so thoughtfully and intentionally is more than potential—it's synthesis realized.

I discuss the pedagogical elements that sustain task potential—such as the opportunities for students to explain their thinking—in the following subsections.

Task Access

The ultimate goal of task potential is to balance rigor and simplicity—that is, what we ask students to know and do should be rich but also accessible. Such a task is referred to as having a low floor, high ceiling (LFHC; Papert, 1980). *Low floor* means the entry point to engaging the task is accessible to all learners, including those who are new to the problem or problem solving. *High ceiling* refers to a range and richness that enables students to develop multiple extensive and complex claims in response to the task. The combination of low floor and high ceiling offers flexibility and fluidity that ensures all have access to ambitious instruction.

Imagine you are teaching a middle school earth and space science course. Consider the problem, *What is the future of manned spaceflight?* Students do not need to understand, say, Einsteinian physics to begin to answer this question (though some students may be able to apply the basics of the theory of relativity—pointing out later in the inquiry process, for instance, that the inability to develop faster-than-light travel may limit man's potential to engage in interstellar travel). Between the texts in the set—which may contain excerpts from NASA plans, articles on the subjects from futurists, illustrations of future spacecraft concepts, and even some science fiction—and students' own research, a number of avenues are available to develop a response. With guidance from the teacher, students may also choose to design their own product, be it a proposed time line or future mission or a letter to the head of NASA.

The previous example suggests several key elements of task access, not the least of which is the differentiation—in pace, in process, in depth—sustained across the learning design. LFHC tasks are characterized by the modest or minimal background knowledge demands required to enter and engage the task, not because the task is dumbed down but because the problem is highly open ended and relevant and the texts in the set provide the needed information to craft a unique but evidence-based response. These resources enable students to engage the task and supporting activities at their entry or readiness level, with plenty of flexibility on how to navigate the task; because the focus of the activities are generative (rather than merely procedural), the opportunity for conceptual surprises increases (English, 2017). As the example also conveys, the creation of a task accessible to all learners does not remove the need for direct teacher support. On the contrary, support becomes imperative to the success of the task. To ensure all students have access to higher levels of cognitive demand, teachers need to provide pathways and scaffolding for students to use when engaging with guiding questions and problems, including individual coaching or conferring, small-group instruction, intentional grouping, modeling, and so on.

I build task access into the lesson structure I describe in this chapter (see Organizing Ambitious Instruction, page 83), and I offer guidance on facilitating instruction in the next chapter (chapter 4, page 113). Task access is in everything you do to plan and enact instruction, and you should not approach it as a discrete feature. Everything is interconnected here: provide a range of access points to students and maintain this level of support and challenge, and meaningful effort emerges during the problem-solving process, including rich discourse among students and between students and the teacher. The key is projecting and planning for multiple pathways and being intentional about how you can assist a range of learners on their intellectual journeys.

Inquiry Space

I've referred to inquiry throughout the book, alluding to it as the logical and best form for ambitious instruction. As complicated as it can be to enact, the underlying concept is quite straightforward: *inquiry* is simply answering problems through an active, exploratory process of analyzing data. The problems are likely to be those you create for students (see the previous chapter); *data* here merely refers to the texts—because it's not always or necessarily numbers—used to answer the problem or question. As George Hillocks (2010) notes, the curiosity and conflict of such data, particularly when viewed in concert with one another, spawn new questions and claims. Attempts to answer these questions become grounds for further investigation and new hypotheses. But don't sleep on the *active, exploratory process* part of inquiry. How we sequence, pace, and differentiate the inquiry so learning is both accessible and authentic is nearly as important as what we ask students to learn or do.

What makes inquiry inquiry—or what makes some inquiry instruction more inquiry-y than others—is based on the level of control and choice that we delegate to the students and the processes that they sequence and enact to answer the problem. This is called the *inquiry space*: the degree to which a task situation enables and shapes students' questioning, problem solving, knowledge application, and so on. The more expansive and fluid the inquiry space, the more likely students are to be engaged and motivated in the task and their learning (Guthrie & Klauda, 2014; Litman & Greenleaf, 2018). (Note that I didn't necessarily say open-ended: *expansive and fluid* can refer to the texts or content engaged, the opportunities for students to discuss or debate with one another, and the products. In other words, you want your inquiry space to encompass whatever will support students creating or composing multiple interpretations and approaches to a problem.)

Table 3.1 defines and delineates levels of inquiry, moving from least to most student agency in the inquiry space; the task situation from the beginning of the chapter guides examples from each level.

Table 3.1: Levels of Inquiry

Level of Inquiry	Definition	Sample Activities
Confirmation Inquiry	Students confirm a concept or principle through an activity in which the results are known in advance or limited to a small set of possibilities.	Students read two articles and a visual display of data on why communism failed in order to identify the three major causes behind the fall of the Soviet Union.
Structured Inquiry	Students investigate a teacher-presented question through a prescribed procedure or process; the teacher and texts may also present multiple hypotheses that the students test and evaluate using teacher-directed procedures.	Students are tasked to solve the guiding question (*How should history view the Soviet Union?*) by analyzing the viewpoints of several authors; in groups, they construct a claim and later defend it in a whole-class debate.
Guided Inquiry	Students investigate a teacher-presented question using student-designed and -selected procedures; the teacher and texts may also present multiple hypotheses that the students test with their own methods.	Students generate and share hypotheses to the guiding question; they then propose a way of testing the hypothesis and form self-selected groups to pursue an answer.
Open Inquiry	Students investigate topic-related questions that they formulate through student-designed and -selected procedures.	Students formulate new questions on the Soviet Union based on interest and then design an inquiry process to determine answers.

Source: Adapted from Bell, Smetana, & Binns, 2005; Litman & Greenleaf, 2018; Rezba, Auldridge, & Rhea, 1999.

I should note that a module can include all the forms of inquiry that we see in table 3.1. Some have suggested sequencing modules to gradually expose learners to each level, with increasing ownership of the inquiry process and product directed to students over time (Zion & Mendelovici, 2012). That said, in this chapter I default to forms of structured or guided inquiry as the standard for ambitious instruction. I do so for two simple reasons: (1) there is evidence that students learn more content-area knowledge and skills with more disciplined inquiry rather than inquiry with a more open structure (though the open structure is expansive when it comes to encouraging diverse student interpretations; Blanchard et al., 2010; Litman & Greenleaf, 2018; Mourshed, Krawitz, & Dorn, 2017), and (2) structured—and, to a lesser extent, guided—inquiry is a much more accessible form of instruction for teachers and students who are not already routinely engaged in the inquiry learning process. A balance between teacher-directed and guided student-directed learning best supports students' deep content learning, providing the appropriate scaffolds to build and leverage background knowledge, inquiry and collaboration methods, and student independence.

As you can see from table 3.1 (page 75), in structured inquiry, the teacher provides students with a problem to investigate, as well as the procedures and materials; students shape the learning outcomes. Structured inquiry is linear. It typically begins with framing the question or problem, moves on to collecting and analyzing the data, and concludes with students drawing conclusions and making claims. To support the process, students receive explicit, step-by-step instructions on how to problem solve; they may even get additional scaffolds—for example, question prompts, organizers, visuals or diagrams, and so on.

Guided inquiry maintains teacher conception and control over the problems or guiding questions, but students, in concert with one another, devise or decide both the outcomes and the processes to follow. Guided inquiry is often not linear. The teacher can make some decisions to focus the learning environment and procedure—for example, that the process will take the form of a lab experiment, or that students should use an established set of texts—but students lead the inquiry process. The teacher may not anticipate the conclusions that students generate. To support the process, the teacher functions as a coach, working alongside students to go through the process, call upon different strategies or approaches, and question emerging understanding.

While the notions of structured and guided inquiry arose out of a desire to align science instruction more closely to the practices of actual scientists, research has shown the inquiry process—namely, analyzing data to construct arguments in response to common subject-area issues—among subject-matter experts is quite consistent across disciplines (Goldman et al., 2016; Moje, 2015). This is not to suggest there are few material and procedural differences between subject areas—think of the prominence literary texts would play in English or substances in science—nor is it to diminish or disavow disciplinary literacy, as building student fluency with the vocabulary, genres, procedures, and so on of your subject remains vital. Rather, I want to make clear that inquiry-based instruction is a concrete and accessible pedagogy. Any subject matter, with nearly any content, can do it. Think of it as a combination of disciplinary literacy and *disciplined* inquiry. The latter is the systematic and coherent ways in which teachers enact the inquiry process in order to support student engagement in the literacy practices of the given subject area.

Take a look at table 3.2, which compares inquiry processes across science, English, and social studies (plus a generic model for all subjects). Note that the phases of inquiry—Initiating Action, Testing, and Concluding—are my own ways of organizing the steps; the descriptions come from the authors.

Table 3.2: Comparison of Common Inquiry Models

Stage		All Disciplines: Four E (Moje, 2015)	Science: Five E Model (Bybee et al., 2006)	English (Elish-Piper et al., 2014)	Social Studies (NCSS, 2013)
Initiating Action	Launch	*Engage*—Frame problem.	*Engage*—Pose question or problem; identify students' prior knowledge.	*Engage*—Introduce essential question and initiate engagement with accessible texts.	*Develop*—Articulate questions and plan inquiries.
Testing	Inquire	*Engineer or Elicit*—Work with and interpret data.	*Explore*—Students engage content to test or construct hypotheses and models.	*Explore*—Read complex texts closely to identify key ideas and themes.	*Apply*—Comprehend and explain disciplinary concepts in sources.
	Cohere	*Examine*—Analyze, synthesize, and summarize findings related to problem posed.	*Explain*—Students explain emerging understanding of concepts to one another.		
Concluding	Assess	*Evaluate*—Interrogate and evaluate one's own claims and those of others.	*Evaluate*—Formally and fully answer the problem or guiding question; self-assess learning.	*Expansion*—Synthesize and integrate understanding from multiple texts.	*Evaluate*—Use evidence from sources to make claims.
	Publish or Present	*Communicate*—Report on claims orally and in writing.	*Extend*—Apply or elaborate concepts and skills in a new situation, resulting in deeper understanding.		*Communicate*—Share conclusions and take informed action.

Source: Bybee et al., 2006; Elish-Piper et al., 2014; Moje, 2015; NCSS, 2013.

To summarize table 3.2, let's synthesize the patterns into a quick four-step recap of what is clearly a shared process across disciplines.

1. Teachers introduce students to the problem or investigation and orient them to it through activation and analysis of their current or prior knowledge of and on it.

2. Teachers guide students as they explore a set of data on the problem and task them with comprehending and constructing key features and concepts within the data.

3. Students engage one another and their ideas in order to explain their reasoning and develop claims or conclusions.

4. Students solidify these claims independently, whether through writing, speaking, performance, or a combination.

It should be noted that not every investigation will proceed in this order and through these components; it may also be the case that students repeat components throughout (for example, students compose and communicate throughout an investigation). But this is the template that is likely to launch most of your investigations. After all, it's what guides the work of your discipline.

If the pattern across frameworks didn't confirm it, let me say it very clearly: inquiry is not a radical idea. Indeed, a seminal report from the National Research Council (Bransford, Brown, & Cocking, 2000) confirms that the foundations of high-quality teaching are the same as what I just described: teachers must frame what students should learn, address and leverage students' preconceptions, provide the cognitive tools and processes to engage the work, and give students multiple opportunities to apply fledgling knowledge and skill learning in order to internalize it. Inquiry *is* good teaching—when implemented effectively, of course. And as noted earlier in this section, effective inquiry is not merely structured or guided; it is *disciplined*. It is rigorous, systematic, coherent—applicable to most instructional situations, and, when taught and supported appropriately, improves student understanding of content, skill, and performance.

Interactive Argumentation

In light of the semantic push by the Common Core—and the Next Generation Science Standards (NGSS) and the C3 and your state standards—away from persuasion and toward argumentation, it can often appear that everything's an argument. Ask students to write a thesis or opinion statement? Argument. Read closely to find evidence in support of a position? Argument. Participate in a debate? Argument. Given the vagaries of what argumentation is and what it should look like, it shouldn't be surprising to hear that significant variation exists in how teachers teach argumentation, even when teaching the same content or practices (Bloome, 2015; Newell, Beach, Smith, & VanDerHeide, 2011).

Let's start with what it is not. It's not *evidence extraction*—that is, asking students to gather a bunch of evidence to support a provided claim. Even situations in which we ask students to develop a claim and provide supporting evidence are often limited argumentation-wise. This forces students to take pre-established or narrow positions and offers few opportunities to challenge prevailing notions or develop new or alternative perspectives (Litman & Greenleaf, 2018). Such a narrowing of the inquiry space is associated with low levels of cognitive engagement and may hinder student learning (Litman & Greenleaf, 2018; McNeill & Knight, 2013).

In this book's definition, *argument* is not merely establishing a claim and providing evidence from text or data; it is a kind and level of thinking in which students grapple with conflicts, perspectives, values, and implications of multiple sources. By this definition, argument is about engagement, not just evidence; it is about synthesis, not just sense making. This skillful, expansive notion of argumentation demands that students:

o Evaluate and contextualize multiple texts for coherence, completeness, and quality

o Recognize, take on, and create multiple perspectives

o Construct and defend interpretations based on evidence, incorporating opposing arguments

o Develop alternative solutions or hypotheses to problems

By design, this definition positions argumentation as a form of evaluation and synthesis; students create through critical engagement with a meaningful array of data.

The pedagogical implications are significant but not inaccessible. Baruch B. Schwarz (2009) delineates the teaching of argument into two types: (1) *learning to argue*, in which instructional support and tasks focus on students learning the language, structure, and principles of argumentation, and (2) *arguing to learn*, in which instructional support and tasks focus on students constructing arguments in order to learn core disciplinary knowledge. To visualize the concept, look at the bullet points describing argumentation in the previous paragraph. Try to imagine a classroom in your subject area in which the teacher explicitly teaches and practices one of these elements versus one in which students explore a problem and evaluate different perspectives on the issue, create an alternative solution, and so on.

With the emphasis on formal argumentation embedded in the Common Core or on the performance assessment of your state tests, it should hardly surprise you to know that much of teachers' instructional focus is on learning to argue. Think of the time you spend on teaching students *claims-evidence-reason*, five-paragraph essays, and so on (Newell et al., 2011). Now that you're well into this book, however, you should also not be surprised that the recommended guidance here is to incorporate both learning to argue *and* arguing to learn. There is emerging evidence that a dual focus deepens students' content knowledge and their capacity to construct arguments (Litman & Greenleaf, 2018). It's the everything, all-of-the-time approach. Provide the opportunities to engage in rich subject-area problems and problem-solving processes; provide the direct instruction to show them how to do these problems and processes. If we don't, we run the risk of limiting inquiry to providing evidence to support a predetermined claim (for example, one explicitly stated in the text or by the teacher). We may also limit student claim generation to superficial or misconceived understandings of core disciplinary concepts. Neither provides the induction into argumentation—nor your subject area—students need for college and career.

This requires more thoughtful, more ambitious instruction in terms of how to teach argumentation, hereafter called *interactive argumentation*. The foundational pedagogies underlying interactive argumentation are straightforward enough. Students ought to routinely work collaboratively (in partners, in small groups, in the whole class) to create arguments with and respond to the arguments of others— argument through interaction, in other words (Chinn & Anderson, 1998). It's easy enough to imagine this in action. Think of students fully engaged in rich reading, discussion, and writing in response to powerful ideas. Putting your teacher lens on, also think of the components necessary to make such collaborative problem solving work: purposeful, structured tasks; a strong focus on engaging texts *as* instruction; individual and group accountability; and multiple opportunities to discuss, debate, and write—in other words, a well-designed inquiry space (Goldman et al., 2016). Not surprisingly, interactive argumentation rarely emerges without significant planning and intentional instructional support (Schwarz, 2009).

Multi-Text Integration

Though we do it every day as literate, knowing adults, the act of comprehending multiple texts on the same or similar topic requires capacities in selecting, analyzing, evaluating, integrating, and communicating that are not tacitly or intuitively available to adolescent students. In fact, these capacities are unlikely to exist at all unless we deliberately and explicitly teach them. It is also exceedingly difficult to design and teach these skills, which may explain why so few opportunities for synthesis are evident in most secondary curricula, and why so little instructional time is spent on reading across texts (Greenleaf & Valencia, 2017). The prevalence of lecture, superficial evidence extraction activities, teacher-driven discussions—these traditional instruction forms result from failure to understand or fear of facilitating academic reading and student-driven inquiry. But have no fear. With structure, smart direct instruction, and feedback, it is very possible to make working with multiple sources work.

Let's start by getting on the same page. Comprehending multiple texts is the construction of coherent meaning from a set of texts that present consistent, complementary, or conflicting information on the same situation, issue, or phenomenon (Bråten, Braasch, & Salmerón, 2017)—synthesis, in other words. Makes sense, right? Because information relevant to solving the problem is scattered across multiple documents instead of being present in one location only or stated explicitly, readers must discover relationships and draw inferences of their own creation. *Integration* is the doing that takes place in the teaching and learning during this undertaking. It's the set of processes—that is, organizing, connecting, and combining information from different texts—that leads students to form connections between the sources, achieve the learning targets, and solve the investigation or problem. Such integration is active and constructive, ultimately seeking to transform those texts into new products of understanding, such as comparison between or among texts, lists or graphic organizers of key ideas from the texts, a hypothesis based on the texts, and so on (Boscolo, Arfé, & Quarisa, 2007; Segev-Miller, 2007).

Integration is iterative and messy, but it has a general flow, one that will inform the instructional guidance in the next section. Typically, it begins or is preceded by understanding the task or problem guiding the textual readings. In most cases, students individually read and process texts first before attempting to combine information from across texts. Obviously, learners cannot internalize and retain the entirety of even a single text, particularly when there are multiple texts to process. To understand the content and achieve the instructional aims, then, readers must prioritize or select information, applying a focus or set of criteria in order to identify ideas unique to single texts, those shared across multiple texts, and those in conflict with one another (Barzilai, Zohar, & Mor-Hagani, 2018; Britt & Rouet, 2012). As they move across texts, learners must additionally recognize and leverage overlaps and discrepancies or relationships of agreement or opposition among the sources, identifying such interrelationships by comparing key aspects of individual texts, continuously linking source to source, and engaging in discourse with peers on the texts (Barzilai et al., 2018; Stadtler, Bromme, & Rouet, 2018).

For obvious reasons, students need strong instructional support to succeed in this process; otherwise, they are liable to utilize single texts and demonstrate partial understanding or misconception of major concepts (James et al., 2014). While integration may be different and more demanding than typical single-text interaction, the inherent pedagogies are the same and include collaborative discussion and practice, annotation of individual texts, and use of graphic organizers—all, as you would expect, are common instructional strategies. The difference, as I will make clear in the next section, is in structure and support. Teachers will need to be intentional about how they sequence the inquiry and the tools they position to help sustain it. Just look at the example from the start of the chapter: it has very high-task potential in terms of its problem and texts, but because the teacher does little to guide students through the inquiry, the students then learn and accomplish little.

The shift for teachers, then, is less about methodology and more about the level of care necessary when implementing common instructional practices, in particular how they launch and sustain investigations. Research on multi-text integration, for instance, has consistently shown that explicit instruction on how to integrate sources—particularly through modeling—can significantly improve student outcomes during independent practice portions of a task (Barzilai et al., 2018). However, intentional direct instruction is one of the hardest elements of good teaching, and thus the component least likely to be taught or executed well. It is an integral part of the approach I describe in the next section.

One key takeaway from the foundational components that I have described is that we cannot reduce the practice of ambitious instruction to a single component. A complex text alone can't achieve rigor; a task with a high DOK alone can't achieve rigor. What's necessary is a multidimensional mindset and approach that help us pinpoint exactly what we need, and what we need to do, to up the standard in our teaching and student learning. Table 3.3 connects those dots.

Table 3.3: The Key Components of Rigorous Tasks

Task Potential

- Task addresses multiple standards, including and especially the integration of knowledge and ideas and research to write.

- Texts meet quantitative, qualitative, and reader or task demands for the grade or course.

- Activities align with expectations articulated in state speaking and listening standards.

- Performance expected of students is not only at or above grade-level standards but also that of what's expected on assessments (for example, PARCC or the SAT).

- Task enables and demands students to engage in core disciplinary ideas and practices.

- Task is problem oriented, requiring students to argue and synthesize from multiple sources in order to address problem.

- Task prompts use of multiple literacies: reading, thinking, writing, speaking, and so on.

Multi-Text Integration	**Inquiry Space Plus Interactive Argumentation**
• Multiple texts serve as tools and evidence to solve meaningful problems. • Multiple texts are a rich and authentic source of disciplinary ideas that encourage close reading and extended discourse. • Multiple texts and instructional support are differentiated so all students have access to complex content.	• Students have multiple opportunities to develop and test their ideas—both with peers and on their own. • Students are repeatedly allowed choice in how they problem solve (for example, in texts, in process, and so on). • Instructional supports include both explicit guidance on complex problem-solving processes and coaching students during practice of them.

With the building blocks in place, let's see investigation in action.

Organizing Ambitious Instruction

Inquiry is a game of interpretation. It begins with curiosity—intriguing but incomplete information or questions that we can begin but not sufficiently answer. Next come the rules of the game, what and how to solve. Participants break down the parts of the problem and fill in the missing information. They engage the game and make initial interpretations. They solicit and respond to input from others. They discuss and debate. Finally, they put forth an interpretation of their own, solving the puzzle.

That's it, in a nutshell, this *investigation*. You may have noticed this term used in the previous chapter to describe the scope and sequence of instructional activities within a module; this was not an accident or mere semantics. Indeed, the choice not to use the word *lesson* is deliberate. The focus is on the problem, not the period—that is, the amount of time your class has each day. Say goodbye to individual or one-off lessons. Our goal instead is to develop a block of instruction—say, between two and six hours of instructional time—that's going to really give learners a chance to explore the guiding question or problem. The length of a given period or lesson is there to help determine how to organize days and times to complete it, of course, but the lesson doesn't end until the investigation does—that is, until engagement with the problem is complete. Beyond reframing instructional time, redefining daily instruction as investigations also helps us attend to the task and teaching components of ambitious instruction. Investigations mean the focus isn't on individual activities but on problem solving; you are supporting and guiding students to think and engage the game critically, rather than simply facilitating lesson components.

What follows is a breakdown of structuring and sequencing investigations, with extensive explanations of each component of the process. A sample application of the method, using the vignette from the start of the chapter, concludes the description. Also included is guidance on how to open up the inquiry so that students are in charge of the process, including an alternative approach to the one I describe in the pages that follow. I recommend having a module or problem in your mind as you go through the steps so you can begin to apply them during or after your review.

Getting Structured Inquiry Right

The structured approach described here relies on *abductive* methods of reasoning—that is, a mix of exploratory (inductive) and directed (deductive) inquiry. Intentional uptake of both inductive and deductive reasoning activities gives students the opportunity to engage in novel and self-directed learning while also having the structures and boundaries necessary to maintain focus, comprehend complex and varied content, and work collaboratively and effectively with others. It's the essence of productive struggle: the *struggle* signifying the students owning the work; the *productive* signifying the teacher creating the structures and boundaries to ensure the struggle is fruitful.

Abductive approaches to teaching have become increasingly prominent in mathematics with the rise of "Upside-down" and "You-Y'all-We" models (Boaler, 2016; Seeley, 2017), both of which flip the traditional gradual release of responsibility model (Pearson & Gallagher, 1983)—in which the teacher demonstrates or leads the work initially, then gradually hands off responsibility for the work through a sequence of collaborative and independent activities—on its head in various ways. They work something like this.

- Students first attempt to solve a challenging problem on their own instead of having a teacher tell them how to solve it—even if students may not be ready to solve it yet (*you* rather than *I* do).

- The teacher, in collaboration with students, refines or guides students' understanding or process through various means—direct instruction, small-group instruction, individual feedback, and so on—and positions students to work together to apply their new awareness and solve the problem, with teacher support (*y'all*).

- The engagement culminates with the whole class (or larger groups) discussing findings from their exploration; the teacher helps draw connections back to the problem (*we*).

More than simply moving parts of a lesson around, abductive forms of instruction shift the role of the teacher from mere facilitator to orchestrator of student discourse, whether during and through problem solving, when organizing students to collaborate, or in guiding a whole-class discussion.

In the model that follows, I have adapted the spirit of this approach to fit the demands of multi-text integration. To make it work when the problem is conceptual or argumentative, and when the data are texts, will require more nimble setting up and launching of the investigation; more structured engagement with the texts to ensure learners can comprehend and critique; and more thoughtful orchestration of whole-group discourse and independent performance. Table 3.4 summarizes each of these components. Detailed guidance on each component follows.

Table 3.4: Components of Structured Inquiry

Investigation Segment	Definition and Key Components
Launching	Previews, diagnoses, and intrigues student engagement and understanding in the investigation; can leverage the problem or a text
Framing	Names the problem, goals and outcomes, and processes guiding the investigation
Positioning	Apprentices students in the problem-solving and content processes and heuristics; teacher may model with students or engage them in shared practice of how to engage in inquiry on the problem
Connecting	Engages students in initial problem-focused reading, comprehension, and evaluation of the texts
Constructing	Engages students in critical rereading and intertextual processing of content, including evidence-based evaluations; construct and test claims
Culminating	Prompts students to independently perform and reflect on the problem, goals, and outcomes guiding the investigation

Note that this structure is meant to be iterative and responsive to learner needs. The order, frequency, and intensity of the components will be determined by the task demands, student needs, and instructional resources (including time). For example, you can repeat parts or prioritize one element over another given the demands of the investigation or learning challenges. You may choose to spend the second day of an investigation remodeling a skill or having students reread a portion of a text, either to fix comprehension gaps or to extend interpretations. You could spend more time on the performing portion, say, if the culminating task demanded it—for example, a more extensive writing assignment, a class debate, and so on. Or you may find it useful to start the investigation midway through an instructional period, implementing only the launching, framing, and positioning portions on the first day; then students could engage in the initial text reads of the connecting component at home before the peer-to-peer collaboration components begin on subsequent days or periods. Adapt, experiment, differentiate—that's the idea.

Again, your total time for an investigation will be somewhere between two and six hours of instructional time, meaning you have multiple days to work with and a great deal of flexibility. Just know that the time and sequence are a baseline, not necessarily an order.

Launching (Five to Ten Minutes)

The initiating action of an investigation should elicit students' generative engagement in the ensuing problem or challenge, positioning students to try and solve the investigation—or some aspect of it—before they are ready, and potentially able, to do so. This may appear counterintuitive, but it serves two important instructional purposes: (1) it cues and intrigues students as to what they will be learning, and (2) it gives the teacher an initial sense of what students know and can do, allowing the teacher to adjust and tailor subsequent instruction based on readiness or interest. A productive beginning is our aim, essentially.

There are three ways of doing so.

1. **Pose the problem:** Perhaps the most obvious approach is to have students engage in low-stakes struggle with the guiding problem itself. Present the question to students, and give them an opportunity, whether individually or with an elbow partner, to propose a solution; a bulleted list at this point is fine. Collect the answers and share with the class; see what patterns, if any, emerge from the data. If fruitful, you can probe students to share how and why they answered as they did.

2. **Evaluate a hypothesis:** In situations where students may struggle to develop an initial response to the problem, or where you may want to cue learners to an alternative or unexpected perspective, you can provide a provocative solution—rather than the ones necessarily expected or desired on the culminating assignment—and have them wrestle with its validity. To do so, conduct a four-square activity, with students going to different corners of the room depending on whether they strongly agree, agree, disagree, or strongly disagree with the statement. After discussing among their peers in the same corner, have a representative from each group share their stance; then, as a class, work together to articulate each stance into a potential claim on the problem.

3. **Preview the texts:** Similar to evaluating a hypothesis, here you would prime students for the investigation ahead by giving them a brief, tantalizing excerpt from one or more of the day's readings. This could be the claim or thesis, a question posed by the author, an example or vignette, or a provocative statement—whatever can serve as a preview of what's

ahead and intrigue your learners. Depending on the content of the excerpt, have students paraphrase it in their own words, discuss with peers whether they agree and how they would respond, and predict what they will learn over the next several days.

After engaging in this pre-inquiry, teachers should take a minute or two to check with students about their prior knowledge or experience on the subject, including beliefs or opinions on the problem. Have students share and see what the range or consensus in the class is. Let them know that self-awareness about our positions is critical for recognizing both our biases and opportunities to expand our perspectives. Have them identify the assumptions or preconceptions they bring to the topic or problem.

There's a simple test to determine how to open an investigation. If you think students can muster a very initial response to the problem on their own, launch with it. If they lack the background knowledge or capacity to initiate the problem, provide the claim or text excerpt that can get them started.

None of this should take longer than ten minutes, and the dividends of orienting students to the content and skills of the investigation will continue to pay off throughout instruction. You can even return to their initial responses at the end of the investigation to compare initial and culminating responses, as well as discuss student progress and areas of growth.

Framing (Three to Five Minutes)

With the initial hook completed, the next step is to give students the lay of the land as to what they will be accomplishing in this investigation. This includes the following.

- The problem
- The skills or content involved in engaging the problem
- The culminating performance upon completing the problem
- Length of time to be provided to complete the investigation, and what students can expect to do over that period
- What you will accomplish on the current day or period

On subsequent days or sessions following the initial launch of the investigation, you can quickly review these elements with students. You may also want to give students a moment to individually set goals and self-assess their progress on elements of the investigation—be it the content or the skills involved.

SIX CONTRARIAN PARAGRAPHS ON LESSON OBJECTIVES (AND NO MORE)

If you've made it this far, you wouldn't be wrong in wondering why, after a whole chapter covering planning and now knee deep in daily instruction, we've focused very little on the role of learning objectives in ambitious instruction.

Don't get me wrong: learning targets are important. They help codify and frame what students should learn in a portion of lesson; they connect individual portions of instruction to the greater whole. When written effectively, they're the task in miniature.

But. Our instinct, because objectives are short and noticeable and changeable, is to make objectives the end all, be all—that is, we don't think we can move forward improving instruction until we fix what's written on the whiteboard. We obsess over single sentences; we create rubrics or go on learning walks to judge the verbs on a whiteboard. I've seen schools spend months—even a full year—of professional development not working on improving student engagement and quality of work just so they could get objectives "right." Most times, they don't.

Here's a radical thought: maybe it's okay that your objectives aren't great. That's not to suggest we want crappy learning targets—but maybe if we're close enough, and if the task and the performance (and performance criteria) are good, we've got something to build on, and we can keep our professional learning focus on what's happening when teachers and students interact. Improving the design and facilitation of the task will improve clarity and coherence of objectives far more than discrete attention to writing them.

The easiest way to get there: align our objective statement to the principles of ambitious instruction. Remember what we said in the introduction? Rigor is nothing but teaching and learning that meets the grade-appropriate standard; ambitious instruction is about constructing meaningful engagement and performance with rigorous subject-area content. It's all right there:

> *the skill or conceptual demands of the standard + the specific content to be learned + performance or demonstration of the standard and content*

If we were to write an objective for the investigation described at the beginning of the chapter, then, it might look something like this: *Students will be able to evaluate in writing the legacy of the Soviet Union by synthesizing treatments from multiple sources on the USSR's successes and failures.* The standard, in this case RH.9–10.9 from the

Common Core—"Compare and contrast treatments of the same topic in several primary and secondary sources" (NGA & CCSSO, 2010)—is addressed by the "synthesizing treatments from multiple sources" component; the content is derived from the language of the task guiding the investigation (i.e., "legacy of the Soviet Union," "USSR's successes and failures"); the performance is captured by "evaluate in writing." One draft writing here: simply tie your problem or investigation to the language of the standards being addressed; mix vigorously.

Positioning (Seven to Twelve Minutes)

One of the more incessant drumbeats of this book is that while inquiry has been repeatedly shown to enhance student engagement and understanding (Shernoff & Bempechat, 2014), it is not an established or comfortable practice in schools—for neither teachers nor students. When you combine that with the increase in rigor of the content—and content engagement—proposed in the book, the threats to sustaining task potential are significant. We need to navigate the inquiry space deliberately, with strong attention to the resources and tools students will need to do sophisticated intellectual work. Some of that will need to be direct instruction.

But only a certain kind of direct instruction will do, one integrated with and integral to the inquiry. That means decisions about when and how to provide direct instructional support will need to arise out of an understanding of the task demands and task access—what students need to know and do to solve the problem, and what they need to be able to do so. As you review this portion, keep that in mind: it's not simply that students need support, it's that they need specific support to do specific tasks or demonstrate specific understanding. The best way to determine that level of support is to solve the problem yourself, using your own expert response to determine the components of mastery response and the key teaching points and predict how students are likely to respond given their present level of readiness. The gap between expectation and present state should give you some ideas as to where you can address existing or likely student learning challenges.

Take a look at the steps you took when you did the task yourself, and compare or consider them against one or both of the following: what you anticipate student responses will be on this investigation and student work from previous instruction. Look at what students are doing (or likely to do) vis-à-vis the challenging content or process in the task, identifying a clear teaching point about *what* to model. Use your thinking steps to guide *how* you model.

The type of inquiry I propose in this book does have commonalities and shared traits that transcend content or task, however, and we can prepare for and integrate them into long-term plans. To help, I've organized likely student learning needs into four categories: (1) *academic reading and writing*, which address the skills students need for multisource integration; (2) *evaluation and argumentation*, which support students' ability to generate claims about what they're learning; (3) *content and concept*, which focus on providing students with the background or academic vocabulary knowledge necessary to engage in the investigation; and (4) *inquiry methods*, which focus on engaging in the problem-solving approaches of an investigation. I describe each in the following subsections, along with guidance on how to organize and deliver the instruction in a way that sets students up to own the effort thereafter.

Academic Reading and Writing

Academic reading and writing skills center on students knowing what to look for—and how to look for it—when processing, integrating, and responding to multiple texts. When positioning reading and writing as a kind of problem solving, teachers show students how to understand individual texts, connect across texts, and draw conclusions to resolve the problem guiding the investigation. Skills involved in such work include the following.

- Recognize and utilize the structures, conventions, and practices of specific text types or genres (for example, how to read science research or how to use sourcing information when reading a historical document).

- Annotate or summarize for specific purposes.

- Integrate multiple texts, such as identifying when texts are in conflict with one another.

- Use fix-up strategies when comprehension falters while reading difficult texts.

This is not an exhaustive list of possible skills, but you get the idea. We're trying to set students up to be productive readers and writers—and problem solvers—when reading texts independently or with peers.

As academic reading and writing skills are need areas that students should practice as they read and write, in most cases you'll want to frontload student engagement with texts by modeling the important academic reading practices *with* them. I emphasize *with* because this demonstration should be interactive, engaging students in the thinking processes you're teaching while guiding them toward enacting the practices independently. Figure 3.2 illustrates the steps and an example of such a process, using the metacognitive strategy of suspending judgment. (Besides being a skill relevant across multiple subject areas, think about how it could support students' ability to create more sophisticated evaluations and arguments about what they read.)

Step	Example
Name the Move (using language from your standards)	Teacher: "Many of you are familiar with the problem guiding this investigation; you may even have heard and formed opinions about it already. This experience or knowledge can be helpful in helping us make connections and draw conclusions, but studies have shown that people tend to have a 'belief bias' on familiar topics that makes it difficult for them to expand their understanding and, thus, learn. Since our learning standards require you to be able to articulate knowledgeable claims and incorporate multiple perspectives in order to reach consensus, we need to make sure we're engaging ideas openly and fully, deliberately seeking to validate our understanding rather than our opinion—that is the core of creating an argument. "To engage in this suspension of judgment, we need to create a focused understanding of what we are reading. Here are the steps we're going to utilize to do so. 1. Create a quick synopsis of what the texts are claiming or conveying. 2. Identify the evidence and reasoning in support of the argument of each text. 3. Identify similarities and differences with the other text (or your prior knowledge). 4. Determine areas where further reconciliation, discussion, or interpretation is needed. "This approach will set us up to take more sophisticated positions on the problem."
Model the Move	Teacher: "Let me show you how to withhold judgement; I will use the political cartoon in front of you. Watch me as I go through the first two steps of the process, taking notes on the features that I do, and writing down the thinking steps I explain; I will call out each step I take." *Teacher then proceeds to do a think-aloud on the text.*
Discuss the Move	Teacher: "What did you notice about what I did to refrain from making immediate assessments of the text?" *Students name what they saw and heard.*

Source: Adapted from Wilson, 2012.

Figure 3.2: Sample interactive modeling for withholding judgment. continued →

Step	Example
Practice the Move Together	Teacher: "Now I want you to try it out. Review the new political cartoon in front of you; when ready, turn to the person sitting next to you and discuss what the text is claiming or conveying and the evidence and reasoning in support of the argument of each text. Remember to use the same questions I did—What is the author trying to say? How do I know?—and note your answers where you find the evidence in the text."
	Students work together to complete the activity; the teacher moves around the room, providing individual feedback where needed.
	Teacher: "To complete the remaining steps of withholding judgment, we just need to compare our notes on each individual text and use that to assess their relationship. Let's start with similarities and differences. What do we notice about what is similar and different about the two cartoons?"
	Students answer.
	Teacher: "Now that we have some ideas about different perspectives on the topic, we're ready to start thinking about what to do with them. A good place to start is by identifying what is resolved—that is, what we still don't know, or what's in conflict, or what's unsatisfying or missing. Return to the guiding problem and ask yourself, 'What do I need in order to respond or what's impeding me from taking a stance on this problem?' Again, we're withholding judgment, so we don't want to answer it just yet; our goal is to find out what else has to be done to answer proficiently. Let's try it together first, and then you'll discuss in groups."
	Teacher solicits and provides feedback on one or two ideas from students; then he or she moves students into groups of four to practice.
Provide Feedback and Next Steps	Teacher: "Nice work making connections across the texts. When breaking into small groups next, be sure and focus on making sure you've resolved the relationships between the texts before generating an initial claim in response to the problem."

A similar and similarly relevant approach is known as *cultural modeling* (Lee, 2007). As with interactive modeling, you launch direct instruction by identifying the problem and previewing the complexity in the texts or tasks. Walk through the steps, questions, or patterns students should engage in just as noted, and process the strategy with students just the same way, too. The difference comes when you practice: rather than practicing with a text in the text set, students first engage a text typical of the kind they interact with or create outside of class—for example, song lyrics, videos, tweets, and so on (hence the *cultural* part). (Note: For obvious reasons, this cultural text needs to contain, exhibit, or require the features or practices you're teaching students to notice or do.) The next step will always be to apply what they're learning to the focus texts of the investigation.

These two modeling approaches are applicable to most areas or skills that students need prior to reading and writing texts; I note where in the subsequent categories.

Evaluation and Argumentation

These two areas address student needs in the areas of interpreting readings and translating that interpretation into claims. You can rather messily divide them into learning-to-argue and arguing-to-learn categories. Argumentation refers to teaching the specific formal skills (as follows) of creating claims and using evidence. Evaluation refers to the teaching of criteria or models to make judgments. In the case of the former, students might need direct support in several of the areas of the expanded definition of argumentation introduced earlier in the chapter (page 79).

○ Developing evidence-based positions

○ Taking on and developing other perspectives or alternative solutions

○ Responding to or rebutting counterarguments

○ Organizing a written (or oral) argument

Many of these argumentation skills will likely require direct instruction methods as does the interactive and cultural modeling described in the Academic Reading and Writing section.

For evaluation, the goal is to teach students a set of criteria or heuristic by which they can assess the quality of others'—or their own—arguments. For instance, a teacher could walk students through, say, three features by which to measure the quality of an argument, or a set of steps to check and assess the reliability of a source. Teachers can also utilize criteria or models from a text source to guide students' ability to evaluate the qualities or merits of what they are studying—say, an excerpt naming the elements of a tragic hero.

When teaching evaluation skills, I like to conduct a quick smell test to assist students in enacting the criteria or model. I start by introducing the guidance to be applied, having students review descriptions of those components; I then conduct a think-aloud with a clear example and nonexample of the criteria or model, walking through how I applied the criteria or model to the case. With the class as a whole, you can then either present several quick examples—some of which you can draw from outside what the students are reading—and see if students assess the examples as meeting the criteria or not, or you can look at specific texts or components of the investigation together and probe students on how they know the criteria apply. When they are ready to fly on their own, task them to use the criteria or model on the texts of the module and see what it elucidates in terms of an answer to the investigation.

Content and Concept

I believe that lecturing should always be an act of last, intentional resort. In nearly all instructional situations where students require additional or extensive background knowledge, a short text that conveys the same or similar information—even one you compose—will always be preferable to a PowerPoint presentation or lecture notes. The reason is self-evident: reading is simply a more active, cognitively demanding process than receiving information. In such situations, the teacher can have students read the text independently or with a partner, with students identifying information in the text they feel will be important to responding to the investigation; the teacher can afterward say again what information students should attend to in subsequent instruction.

But there may be situations where a problem or the texts require foregrounding that you can't convey more clearly or quickly through texts, and that is when a brief, interactive lecture can assist. Keep the following pointers in mind.

- State what the lecture will accomplish or answer in the form of a question (for example, *What is a tragic hero? What caused the Cold War between the United States and Russia?*).

- Explain why it is important to know this information and how it connects to or supports the investigation.

- Provide or have students construct a graphic organizer that can help them organize their notes during the lecture (for example, a chart with columns or a table for comparison and contrast, or a list with steps for them to record a process).

- Facilitate a pausing point where students can reflect on and ask questions about what they've learned.

- When finished lecturing, have students pair up with a partner to answer the guiding question of the lecture in their own words.

- As a segue, explain again how the lecture connects to what students will do during the investigation.

This should take no longer than five to ten minutes.

Inquiry Methods

There may also be a need to walk through how to engage in the activities of an investigation at the expected level of performance. For instance, students will need to learn how to engage in and sustain high-level conversations in both small- and whole-group discussions, necessitating guidance on how to ask and respond to questions from peers, how to utilize evidence, and so on. Direct instruction may also be warranted in setting up classroom norms and routines, such as that at the outset of a period and without waiting for instructor prompting, students will work with an elbow partner to begin to answer the problem. Or perhaps written responses at the culmination of the investigation should be of an expected length or form. You can apply the same interactive modeling process described earlier to these need areas as well.

It's worth noting again that guiding and directing students can and should occur at any time they need a model of expert practice in order to do more rigorous work; it does not necessarily have to be at the start of an investigation or even of a day or period. As you'll see in the detailed example later in the chapter (page 102), positioning can also occur multiple times in an investigation, and for different skills and purposes. It all depends on what students need, and when they need it. The simple rule is this: positioning should foreground and serve as guided practice to those skills students will need support for in order to collaborate or act independently.

Connecting (Forty-Five to Ninety Minutes)

At first glance it may seem prudent to focus initial student engagement with texts purely on comprehension. Understandably, the problem and the texts may be complex; there may be a lot to read or write or do during the investigation. Our instinct is not wrong in wanting to make sure students get it before going deeper.

But focusing solely on understanding the main ideas of each text, or even just identifying similarities and differences among texts, is not sufficient to enable synthesis (Kobayashi, 2015). Even at the outset of the investigation, our key goal has to be positioning students to move beyond a mere surface or superficial level of the text, or even across texts, and toward higher-order thinking *during* their reading. Of course, we do want students to understand the gist of the arguments or descriptions that the text provides, but we want them to do so in support of understanding the landscape of the problem they are investigating. Furthermore, we want students to make *connections*—that is, not merely comprehend content but also begin to draw analytical relationships among ideas and in response to the problem.

To do so, initial engagement with the texts needs to position students to engage in three performances concurrently and flexibly: (1) leveraging what they are learning and applying from previous positioning, (2) reading within and across texts for both literal and inferential purposes, and (3) developing understanding through discussion and consensus building. Given these demands and opportunities, the four-part sequence that follows features a significant amount of chunking of tasks, lots of quick and engaging movement between independent and collaborative activity, and plenty of options in terms of how the teacher or students could choose to tackle the texts.

Note: This component of the task is likely to comprise the most instructional time of any in the sequence; it may extend across multiple periods or days. Of course, time on task here will vary based on the number of texts students will read and their complexity, students' readiness and familiarity with the content, performance, and so on—it's an instructional situation–specific decision.

I devised the following four steps that discuss setting up initial engagement.

1. **Preview the landscape:** Provide students with a macro-, high-level understanding of the texts and investigation by looking quickly and briefly at an element of the content that best conveys the range of ideas and issues students will investigate. This can be the launch text or your nonprint source, assuming either is part of the investigation (you can also reread, if relevant). Most likely, however, you'll want to grab short excerpts—a quote or a paragraph, say—from each of the texts. The excerpt you select should be the sentences that capture the ideas in the text most compelling to the investigation. With these blurbs, you'll want to prompt and facilitate students to do two things: (1) be able to restate what each piece is about in their own words and (2) create a quick classification scheme (for example, pro-or-con, common solution or alternative solution) that they can use as a label for each text. The first option gives students a sense of what to expect when they read; the second helps them easily distinguish the texts when reading them in full.

2. **Set up the reading:** Restate the problem or investigation, and explain how students will collect information during reading, such as with annotation, a graphic organizer or note taker, summary, or a visual-spatial diagram. Make clear what students are to capture and how. Specify what students will need to consider as they read the texts and take notes.

3. **Facilitate the initial reading:** For the first engagement with the texts, divide students into pairs and distribute the full texts (if you haven't done so). Let students know that they'll first look more closely at the texts to determine what sorts of conclusions they can draw about the problems. Using the monitoring method you established from the previous step, have students approach the readings in one of the following ways.

   a. *Summarizing*—Students confront each text individually, summarizing each first and then looking across summaries to determine connections. Summaries—whether in graphic organizer form or notes—should include articulation of the main ideas of the text, the evidence provided by the main author, and whether there are observable conflicts or contrasts within the text or with other texts.

   b. *Orbiting*—Students concentrate on one text (likely the most complex or longest from the text set), focusing on breaking down its main ideas and supports. When ready, they read the others as "satellites"—that is, reading to see how they relate to the main text. Students make note of these relationships and inconsistencies.

c. *Focusing*—Students look for a specific idea in or across the texts or to apply a specific process. Here, the students may do an initial skim or scan, identifying and noting relevant components in a given text; they would then switch to another text to identify and compare. For instance, a teacher can assign students to locate where authors state their evaluations of the Soviet Union. Once determined, students return and do a more complete read of the texts.

Note how the use of these strategies can vary depending on student readiness, texts or task, and classroom routines and practices. This component is also ripe for guided inquiry opportunities, as you could position students to choose from among the approaches the one that best suits them. Alternatively, you can also employ a more structured reading protocol (for example, reciprocal teaching) during the reading of the text if it will assist students.

4. **Codify initial relationships and assessments:** Once initial readings are complete, combine pairs into groups of four, and task groups to discuss the following findings: ideas repeated across the readings, differences among the readings, and inconsistencies and conflicts among the readings. Once students have identified these, they should pinpoint what they find convincing, claims and evidence, and what they do not. Students can also identify elements or voices they find to be missing in the texts. Regroup the class as a whole and lead a short discussion around the following questions: *What did you discover while reading or connecting the texts? What reasoning and evidence stood out to you? What's missing?* This is also a good time to check if students have comprehension issues. Solicit their questions and address them by having students look for evidence across the texts to support answers in response.

To determine the order in which to engage texts and the time and focus of the reading, you'll want to consider both the complexity of the text and the utility of the text to solving the problem. Use the relevance and rigor of the texts to determine which of the three options (summarizing, orbiting, or focusing) is best. To determine the tools used to track readings and the prompts, identify what students will need to attend to and leverage in the texts in order to complete the investigation; the method and organization should be based on how students can best extract meaningful information.

Constructing (Thirty to Ninety Minutes)

Once an initial read and understanding is complete, the next step is for students to dig deeper into the meaning of the texts and their implications. The goal is for students to translate their understanding into answers, solutions, and actions in response to the problem. Constructing is more than a bridge to the assessment, it's the space in which students codify their ideas, make their claims, and develop their arguments. Give this step the instructional time it needs and demands.

This component has three parts: (1) reassessing, (2) reframing, and (3) refining. *Reassessment* centers on students articulating what texts—and which portions of them—they find most useful for conceptualizing and solving the problem. The groups of four reread the selections, discussing how the texts add to their understanding and criticism or confusion about perspectives on the problem. You can also complete reassessment by withholding the reading of part or whole of a text in the investigation until this point, or you can have students reread a portion of the texts they already read. What counts most here is the specific nature of the content: it should be something that challenges or extends initial thinking. Students should engage the text just the same as they did the other texts—such as by summarizing findings, raising questions, and so on—but this time they should connect what they're learning back to the problem guiding the investigation: *How does this build our understanding of the problem? How does it address challenges in our initial understanding? How does it challenge that understanding?* Specifically, task students to *qualify*—that is, to not accept any argument (in the texts or their own) without specifying the situations or contexts in which the argument could or could not be true.

The second phase, *reframing*, helps students formulate a response to the problem. To do so, the teacher positions students to formally evaluate stances in response to the problem, using these assessments to construct—or adapt—their own perspectives.

You conduct evaluation, as we discussed earlier in the chapter, by applying a set of criteria or a model to test the alignment of a text's ideas to the established standard. You can supply the criteria or model—see a description of how in the Positioning section (page 89)—by which students should check each text to see how it matches the criteria or model. Students can also generate the criteria or model themselves through and from examining the texts. To do so, have students consider the strengths and weaknesses of each text's argument, looking at both the strongest features and the errors or limitations of each; they should then analyze the patterns, identifying repeating features or ideas identified as strong and arguable.

From here, they should do some or all of the following.

- o Test out the criteria or model (for example, apply it to an additional text or conduct an experiment).

○ Generate equally appealing alternative solutions or perspectives to those in the texts or held by students.

○ Qualify the positions in terms of the conditions in which their arguments or positions are valid or useful (if not fully addressed in Reassessing).

Now synthesis can occur. Having evaluated and tested out their perspectives, students have some data on what works and what doesn't. Their task now is to codify, which they can do by answering the following question: *What is a conclusion or claim or solution that you can put forth that best attends to the strengths, accounts for the weaknesses, and addresses the gaps of what we've read?* In other words, students should map out the perfect argument, the one that addresses both the strengths and nuances they've examined across texts. Have students sketch out an initial position and support. Be flexible about initial language, using words such as "We believe . . ." to introduce their initial positions. Bullet points for denoting supporting evidence are fine to start. Subsequent activities will help refine and formalize their stances.

The third part, *refining*, takes place in a whole-group discussion. Here, the purpose is to position students to test out and respond to emerging ideas in response to the problem. The end goal is to set students up to respond to the problem—or an extension of it—on their own. To do so, set up the whole-group discussion space so that students can bring their emerging understanding and perspectives to the table and so that the engagement among and between peers helps improve and solidify those perspectives. Students have already done the first part in the previous component. What you need to do now is organize the discourse.

I have identified three options for doing so, with the teacher role as leader of the discussion moving from more to less intensive with each successive option. Feel free to combine the following approaches.

1. **Problem space or solution space:** Here the teacher creates a deliberate structure for discussion to ensure students are engaging fully in the problem. First, align students to the complexity of what you are examining. Have them name the problem and summarize the different perspectives or understandings it examines. Ask what has been challenging and conflicting about what they're seeing in the texts, with students noting weaknesses in their own and the texts' arguments. Second, explain to students that as a class you want to find the most reasonable explanation, argument, or solution to the problem—one that aligns with the evidence, meets the criteria or model established, and represents what the class thinks is the best fit. Solicit an initial response to the problem, guiding students to explain the evidence and reasoning in support and how it meets established criteria or guidelines for a sufficient response. Ask other

members of the class to clarify or add on to this claim before soliciting responses to its merit. Repeat as needed. You can seek consensus by continuing to hone a single solution or by soliciting multiple approaches and taking a vote; you can seek irresolution, too, by continuing to collect a desired range of responses. (See next section for why.)

2. **Representation:** This approach uses a set of student responses to launch and guide discussion. There are two ways to take this approach: (1) open and (2) selective. In the open approach, collect all of the responses from the groups of four—you can have students write on the board or enter them onto a shared electronic document—and then do an initial pattern analysis of the responses by having students identify where there are similarities or overlap, or by affinity mapping. If consensus is not immediately evident or there are a range of responses, you can do the four corners activity again. Have students rank and discuss the proposed solutions or create new discussion groups with representation from each perspective. In the selective approach, you would intentionally preselect and sequence one to three student responses around which to build a discussion, using students' ideas to enable them to directly engage one another about their understanding and perspectives. For instance, you could launch a whole-group discussion by first sharing a conclusion that has a misconception or inconsistency, positioning classmates to correct or clarify this error. Once you have resolved this misconception, you can then transition the class to consider a response that may be at odds with or act as an outlier to other responses. Discussion can conclude with examining the most common or frequent response, which will then position students to re-examine established positions.

3. **Debate:** You can debate investigation topics that engender a wide variety of answers, perspectives, or solutions—as issue problems tend to, more so than interpretive problems, while setting up the structure of the back-and-forth but significantly reducing your involvement in facilitation. There are several ways of making this work. The most debate-like is to identify two perspectives on the topic and merge the groups of four so that all students are in a supergroup for one of the perspectives. These students can then listen to and adapt their positions to find consensus. Use the Lincoln-Douglas debate structure—opening, rebuttal, closing argument—to ensure more students can participate. Another approach, drawing from Rogerian argumentation theory, is to have each group share its perspective and reasoning, allowing other groups to question the perspective or change sides as needed. Once groups have shared, the class as a whole can discuss

the needs and values of the various sides and try to reach a compromise solution that meets as many of these needs as possible.

Your unpacking of your own problem solving is critical during the constructing component. Use your understanding of your own problem solving to help illuminate how to help students problem solve. What did you do to connect ideas across texts? What did you do to take a position on or determine a solution to the problem? What would you want to discuss with others in order to share or solidify your position? Answering these questions can help you determine the sequence of activities. If using a set of criteria, the best pathway to defining or devising them is to first consider your own internal metrics and then cross-check them with a reputable source.

Culminating (Twenty to Forty-Five Minutes)

The investigation concludes with students answering or extending the problem independently, either during or outside of class. Often you will ask students to compose a written response directly addressing the problem. However, if the standards assigned to the investigation call for a specific performance or product, or if you're focusing on developing students' skills in a particular facet of academic writing, you can designate unique task parameters—for example, a lab report or the development of parts of the culminating performance assessment. (I discuss the design of this assessment in chapter 2, page 39.)

Assuming you don't already have a planned written product in place, for whole-class group discussion, you'll want to set students up to build on, rather than repeat, what they know and believe about the problem, and respond and adapt to their progress. You can do so by prompting students to do the following.

o Address any lingering issues, inconsistencies, or challenges that arose or were not addressed (fully) in class discussion.

o Extend an interesting or powerful point that a peer made.

o Develop or take on an alternative perspective on the issue.

o Apply what they learned to related content or an issue (for example, looking at Putin's Russia after the fall of communism).

Early on in students' engagement with the inquiry model, it will make sense to specifically assign one of these prompts. However, as students' familiarity and capacity with the process grows, you can begin to give them more control and choice in terms of how to respond. One suggestion is to make the prompts from the bulleted list the standard options for response and allow students to pick one based on the success of the discussion or their interests.

If students need additional time to read and comprehend the texts, and if whole-group discussion needs to shift to ensure students have a full grasp of the problem, it may be that culmination is simply to have students answer the problem on their own. However, if students accelerate through the problem quicker than anticipated, it will be useful to have these alternative prompts ready, such as responding to a different text or responding to student ideas during the discussion.

Following composition and submission of the response, conclude the investigation by spending a few minutes of instructional time on individual and whole-group unpacking of the learning experience. For the individual component, give students an opportunity to assess themselves according to the grading criteria for the investigation or any established class-level criteria. If nothing else, students should reflect on how well they did in the investigation, including where they experienced growth and where they need additional support or clarity; have them set goals for the next step or future engagement with a similar concept or skill.

The group reflection functions as a process check and wrap-up, which you can facilitate via whole-class discussion. Check with the group to see how their learning is sitting: What questions do they have now? What is still lingering for them? If students composed anything in response to any of the prompts listed on page 101, you could share a few. Wrap up by checking to see how students feel you can improve the learning process.

SEEING IT IN ACTION

Let's consider how the vignette from the start of the chapter would play out if you applied the inquiry model described over these last pages fully and with integrity. Segments of the model appear in bold type. Please note that the school in this example is on a block schedule.

Day 1

Launching: Upon entering the classroom, students see the ongoing investigation problem displayed: *How should history view the Soviet Union?* Once settled, the teacher welcomes everyone and rephrases the problem: "Thinking about everything we've learned about the Cold War and the rise and fall of the USSR, what legacy or lasting understanding is likely for Soviet communism? Remember that when we launch an inquiry into a problem, we start by creating an initial hypothesis or solution. Share your initial thought with your partner and discuss." Students then receive three to five minutes to share and discuss their ideas. The teacher works his way around the room, clarifying the question for those who have trouble getting started.

Once student-to-student discussion wanes, the teacher brings the class back together and asks for several volunteers to share their evaluations. Once they have shared, he asks the class if they observed any patterns in their classmates' responses. After they identify the patterns, he tells the class to hold on to their initial impressions for use later in the investigation.

Framing: The teacher restates the problem, letting students know they'll be spending the next two instructional periods making sense of it by looking at a set of documents on the subject: a political cartoon and two excerpts from analyses by historians on the subject. Students will also be learning how to make evaluations on historical events by applying a set of criteria to judge an event's historical import. At the end of the investigation, students will return to the question the class started with and answer it in full and formally on their own.

Positioning: The teacher revisits context: "Today, however, we really want to be able to understand what perspectives exist already about the legacy of the Soviet Union so that we can begin to form our own interpretations," the teacher says. He notes that the class hasn't discussed how it all came crashing down at the end, so he wants to do a quick overview of the demise of the Soviet Union and why it happened. "The guiding question for the next few minutes will be *What were the causes of the dissolution of the Soviet Union?*" he says. "I'm going to briefly discuss a few of the key causes that led to the USSR's downfall, so I want you to take thirty seconds and create a graphic organizer in your notes that has two columns: one for the causes and the second for connections; make sure you have enough room for four entries." He instructs the class to take down the name and description of each cause he provides and tells them he will explain the connections part shortly.

The teacher notes how economic stagnation was a persistent issue, with high unemployment, scarcity of consumer products, and a large black market that sapped key tax revenue; he also notes how liberalization by the last president, Mikhail Gorbachev, led to Russians being able to freely protest, get access to Western media, and vote—thereby increasing interest in more democratic forms of government. The teacher pauses and asks students to turn to an elbow partner and describe the two causes of the dissolution of the Soviet Union. He also asks students to identify any clarifying questions they have. Once students have responded to these prompts, he tells them the connections column is for them to note relationships and parallels they've learned from previous studies—for instance, how military spending to keep up in the arms race was bankrupting the country and hampering the economy. He gives students a minute to discuss in pairs any connections they can draw and then facilitates a quick sharing session. Next, he shares the final two causes—rising nationalism in satellite states and political turmoil—and again asks students to turn and talk to a partner about what they're hearing and the connections they're making. He solicits clarifying questions. "Understanding why the USSR failed will help us clarify what worked and didn't work about this historical experiment in communism," he says.

Connecting: The teacher distributes the three texts. "As you recall, we always launch a text set by getting a high-level gist of each text," he says. "Let's take a look at what we have today and consider what we can glean about the texts' relevance to the investigation topic." The teacher has students review the political cartoon on their own first and then asks them to restate in their own words what they think the text is saying. He does a quick check for understanding on what students find. Next, on the SMART Board, he displays a key sentence or two from each of the two articles—"Russia's Persistent Communist Legacy" and "Stalin's Death 50 Years On"—and asks students to review and restate for each. Again, they share and clarify with partners. The teacher checks to make sure students have the gist. He then asks students to label each source based on the key idea they notice in each.

The teacher notes they'll be examining the texts more closely now, and to do so they'll need to track both the arguments of each source and the key reasoning and explanations behind them. He asks students to annotate the texts specifically to capture these elements. The class turns to "Russia's Persistent Communist Legacy." The teacher asks students to do an initial read of the two-page excerpt on their own, identifying reasoning and evidence that support the initial understanding they got from looking at the excerpt. When finished, they work with an assigned partner to check each other's findings, returning to specific parts of the text they annotated to share where and what in the text they identified. The teacher circulates and addresses any comprehension breakdowns he observes. The pairs next review the political cartoon together, looking for connections to the first text.

The teacher merges pairs to form groups of four, tasking the groups to share their findings, noting connections and distinctions across the readings. The teacher monitors the groups, encouraging them, when ready, to discuss arguments they find relevant and convincing. He also encourages the groups to share questions or critiques they have about what they read. After about five minutes, the teacher brings everyone back to the whole group and asks the class to share reasoning and evidence in the article that stood out to them. He solicits input from a student who noticed that one of the articles does not deal with the economic failures of the USSR that they discussed prior to reading. He then asks the class what lingering issues or questions they have about the text, clarifying for them what *glasnost* is. With the period winding down, he asks students to review their initial answers to the investigation problem and make two additions or changes based on what they learned. Students submit their responses on the way out.

Day 2

Launching: As class begins, the teacher shows students a smattering of their exit slips from the previous day to remind them of what they learned. He notes patterns in what he observed from student submissions. Next, he shows a sentence from "Stalin's Death 50 Years On," which he notes is the reading that will guide today's work, that conflicts with several students' responses. He asks a student to restate the gist of a perspective.

Connecting: He tasks students to read the full excerpt from "Stalin's Death 50 Years On," annotating for both its argument and reasoning and where it challenges and conflicts with the previous day's findings. When done reading, students return to their groups of four and discuss how this text builds their understanding of the problem. They also discuss the conflicts and opportunities presented by this alternative perspective that they gained through closer examination of the text.

Framing and positioning: The teacher regroups and sets the agenda for the remainder of instructional time: "Today we're going to focus on making critical evaluations of historical events, in this case the Soviet communist state. One of the ways in which historians make such evaluations is by identifying a set of criteria that can help them distinguish whether a situation, or even a state, meets the standard it's set or expected. For instance, there are criteria that historians use to define a functional democracy, such as popular sovereignty—that is, that citizens elect their leaders." The teacher goes on to note that for today's class they'll be using a smell test of what makes a nation-state successful. He notes that while the USSR did collapse, we need to consider what it was able to do during its existence and how that affected the world today. He notes that scholars of history often consider three key features when it comes to the efficacy of a state: (1) its ability to provide and maintain services, most especially security; (2) the ability of its citizens to participate fully and freely in the political process, such as by voting; and (3) its influence—political, cultural, technical, and so on— on nations and peoples within and outside its boundaries. The teacher notes that we can determine the relative quality of a nation by assessing its strengths and weaknesses in each of these areas, with the strongest nations passing the smell test in every category, while weaker nations have more mixed results. "We can use our ratings to pinpoint lasting gains and failures of a country, and thus articulate its legacy," he says. He models by using Canada as an example. He goes through each one of the categories, noting its strengths in the first two categories and its strong national identity, though it may not be assessed for contributing significantly to the rest of the world. Next, he leads the class in guided practice with the United States, soliciting input from the class on each category, pressing students to explain how it addresses those criteria. He explains his thinking.

Constructing: The teacher reiterates the criteria and notes that they're going to use the smell test to make an initial assessment of the USSR, which will then be used to formulate claims about the legacy of the state. He tasks the groups of four to review the readings—and earlier texts, if relevant—for evidence in support or refutation of each of these categories. One student will record their key points of strengths and weaknesses. Students spend a few minutes on their own reviewing all three texts, then share their findings with their group and begin to reach consensus. The teacher moves about the room to check on progress and push student thinking. Once the review is complete, he asks the groups to do a quick assessment in each category and overall and then runs a poll of the whole class, making sure to have students observe how their peers responded. They'll return to the assessments in a few minutes. He tasks groups to turn to the legacy component by reviewing their notes from the evaluation and answering the following question: *What will the Soviet Union communist state be remembered for above all else?* Circulating around the room, he notices one group has a provocative idea emerging—that the legacy of the USSR should be that of providing an alternative, albeit a failed one, to American democracy—and decides to center the whole-group discussion around it. When all groups are ready, he has this group share first, asking the class to consider the evidence for and merits of this perspective, and then has people weigh in on whether it's a fair assessment. After a few minutes of discussion, he has another group share a more conventional argument, and the class discusses how it reflects the evaluation criteria and how it compares to their own arguments.

Culminating: For homework, the teacher has students compose a one-page response to either one of the following: (1) they can pick up a stance from class discussion they found interesting and want to elaborate on or challenge, or (2) they can develop a response to the claim that the legacy of the USSR is as an idea, not what it did or did not accomplish. Students return the next day to class, where the teacher first has them group around their response selections and reflect on their answers. After a few minutes, students return to their desks and write for three to five minutes on what they feel they were able to accomplish in their responses and their growth areas. They submit these reflections with their written assignments.

One of the takeaways from the elaborated model and example is that inquiry is not a hands-off situation for teachers; rather, it offers new opportunities to be intensively involved with students in the meaning-making process. A structured approach like the one detailed in the preceding pages allows for the following outcomes.

- **Sustained problem-based learning:** From start to finish the inquiry model focuses on the guiding problem. Notice how in the example the teacher not only opens and closes the investigation with the problem but returns to it, even and most especially during reading.

- **Sustained attention to students' ideas:** Students are treated as sense makers from the very outset of the investigation, then positioned to be more skilled at sense making throughout the investigation; indeed, the positioning portion is designed to do just that. Notice how in the example the teacher finds opportunities in every component of the instruction to enable student input and to encourage connections. Direct instruction on the second day specifically sets students up to do complex critical thinking.

- **Multiple reads of the texts:** Students interact with the texts multiple times and in multiple ways, from close reads to skimming or scanning, from annotating to leveraging in discussion, and from collaboratively to independently. Notice how in the example students are intentionally exposed to the texts, with a sequence that enables them to both analyze individual texts and compare across texts multiple times over the two days.

- **Multiple methods of teacher support:** The teacher enables and facilitates student thinking in several strategic ways, through questioning, through modeling, through discussion, and so on. Notice how in the example the teacher is a constant presence throughout the inquiry, leveraging a range of methods—lecturing, think-pair-shares, guided practice, small-group support, and so on—to assist students in accessing rich content and complex tasks.

- **Iterative organization:** The model is adaptive, allowing for different permutations depending on period length, student readiness, and need. Notice how in the example the inquiry is stretched out over roughly two and one quarter periods, with some elements of the model—launching, positioning—repeating to account for the multiday investigation and the increased complexity of the task.

A structured approach is not the only way of facilitating inquiry with texts, and you need not use it in every instructional situation. The task potential and task access will dictate how to utilize the inquiry space in such situations. That said, more so than any other approach, the investigation model detailed in this chapter addresses all the components of ambitious instruction—engaging all students, the focus on higher-order reasoning, and the teacher support during instruction—more effectively and flexibly.

Going Guided

One thing you may have noticed from reviewing the structured model is that opportunities for students to direct the inquiry are plentiful and do not require a new structure or approach, in order to make the process more open and student driven. Essentially, you're leveraging the same four elements commonly referred to when differentiating instruction: process, content, product, and environment (Tomlinson, 2003). Strategies for each follow.

- **Take control (process):** Notice how several of the model components have options from which you can choose. You can give students control over how they conduct initial readings or engage in whole-class discussion. Of course, you'll want to spend some time building students' fluency with and awareness of these problem-solving approaches, and gradually ramping up their ownership and independence with the strategies, before allowing them to choose. But in my experience, repeated, deliberate practice will enable them to recognize which approaches best support them.

- **Expand text options (content):** Provide students with a broader range of texts—including the opportunity to return to previously read texts—from which they can choose the resources that best fit their problem-solving method and perspective. When relevant, they can also do research in search of additional texts or evidence.

- **Choose an ending (product):** Provide several response options for students to select from when completing the culminating task—see the list in that section (page 101)—if not the performance assessment. One possible approach is to provide a directed option but always allow for students to respond directly to an idea shared in class or to construct an alternative or counterargument to the prevailing consensus or conclusion.

o **Partner purposefully (environment):** With guidance, students can also select who they work with and how they organize themselves. You can do so by brainstorming with your class on how best to organize for an investigation, and then choose the kind of partners students think are best suited to support their inquiry; together, you can decide when and how to employ this arrangement.

You can employ any combination—or all—of these approaches to make the inquiry more guided. The demands of the investigation, and the readiness of the students, will determine where the opportunities lie.

A more thoroughly comprehensive approach to increasing the openness of inquiry is to flip the structured model on its head, shifting the problem-solving processes toward inductive methods. In such an approach, identifying the problem itself becomes a key part of the learning process. In this case, the teacher's main role is to guide students to select and respond to an appropriate problem or problems, rather than simply dictate what they address. The five-part sequence of learning would look like this.

1. **Connecting:** Students read the texts first, engaging in the same sort of summarizing and relationship defining as in the structured model, only here whole-group discussion functions to help students identify the problems presented by and shared among the texts. The outcome of the discussion should be identifying the one or two problems to be addressed as the investigation. If the problem identified or determined is unlikely to facilitate meaningful inquiry, the teacher can use questioning and feedback to help students self-assess the extent to which the problem addresses the three traits of good problems (see chapter 1, page 18) and then help guide them toward an articulation of a better-suited problem.

2. **Launching:** Students spend some time in small groups framing the problem, such as the complexities of the issue and possible barriers. They brainstorm an initial solution or answer. Groups share their answers.

3. **Framing and positioning:** Students discuss how to test their solutions and agree on the processes for doing so. You can develop criteria for evaluation as part of the process.

4. **Constructing:** Students test out their initial answers—and those of the class or the texts—by using their agreed-on process to return to the texts and develop a more intricate and detailed response to the problem. You

can provide group-specific direct instruction as needed. Groups determine how to share their initial thinking with their peers—for instance, they can jigsaw or do a whole-group discussion—and use the feedback they receive from you and their classmates to adjust their responses.

5. **Culminating:** Students share their findings via a teacher-directed product or process, such as by presenting to the class or a written response.

This process features many of the same principles and practices as the structured model—use of whole-group discussion, for one—but strongly emphasizes student leadership on the process and iteration throughout. Students will need to be ready and willing to hold their peers accountable for this to be successful.

Envisioning the Path Ahead

By now you're no doubt sweating the process—*How will this work? How will I keep students engaged? What happens if some students or groups get stuck?*—but at the outset of your planning and preparation to launch an investigation, I highly suggest you focus on product. That is, know your investigation. Know what you're asking students to do and why. Know what it will mean to be successful during and as a result of the investigation. Know what meaningful, authentic learning would entail for this investigation.

Let me reiterate that the best way to unpack this is to do the task yourself first— that is, before you plan out the specifics of the investigation. Read to teach. Examine the texts and write an exemplar response to the investigation, stopping during reading and writing to identify key mental steps or processes you undertook to complete that component of the work. Note where you had trouble or saw opportunities for intrigue; think about where students will face the same. Think about alternative approaches to the culminating response. Consider how your response will compare to what students are likely to produce without additional support.

To finish where we started, note that my focus has been entirely on maximizing the coherence and quality of inquiry, not on fitting the structure into a period or days of instruction. Only after you've mapped out the student learning trajectory should you then begin to parcel time within and across periods. Once you've got a sense of the demands of the investigation, and once you've got a sense of what it will take for students to realize those demands, you can map it across the number of days necessary. This may open up the opportunity to include additional components—say, a formative assessment or a skills minilesson—to leverage this organization.

How to plan for and provide support to students during these components is the focus of the next chapter.

The Big Idea

It's important to note that the work encapsulated in this chapter does not happen in isolation. Context matters. The learning environment matters. Teacher encouragement and coaching matter. Support from your colleagues and your administrators matters. Keep all this in mind as you review and reflect on what you learned from this chapter.

- Cohering and connecting information across multiple documents and data sources requires deep and fluid inferencing and interpretation skills. Without specific supports and structures around multi-text integration, students will not be able to engage what they read critically.

- Inquiry pedagogy, when structured intentionally to sequence and support student reasoning, enhances student engagement. Using a variety of intentional participation structures (for example, think-pair-share, small- and large-group discussions, or team-based learning) can provide key scaffolds to enable students to do ambitious intellectual work.

- Tasks that address both students' ability to synthesize (learning to argue) and opportunities to synthesize (arguing to learn) are the best suited to addressing students' content, disciplinary literacy, and academic reading and writing skill needs in your subject area.

- Increasing student leadership in driving the inquiry (that is, guided inquiry) does not require a change in the structure or sequence of the structured inquiry instructional model. Rather, you will need to be intentional about how you build students' independence when it comes to managing and regulating their own learning, as well as how they support and lead their peers during learning activities.

Facilitating Ambitious Instruction

The classroom of our ambitious eighth-grade ELA teacher from the beginning of the book is abuzz. Students have spent the last ten to fifteen minutes in mixed groups looking across two texts, an excerpt from *Narrative of the Life of Frederick Douglass* (Douglass, 2014) and the historical fiction novel *Chains* (Anderson, 2008), to determine how the texts establish messages about the human condition—sort of an interpretive and an intellectual problem in one. While students look for evidence to help generate claims—they are to come to whole-class discussion with quotes that exemplify their answers—the teacher moves about the room, holding quick one-to-one conferrals to support their progress and help them integrate the module vocabulary words into their responses. She strategically reconfigures small groups based on the answers she is hearing, allowing for students with various perspectives to intermingle.

When the teacher brings the whole group back together, she opens the floor to any student who wants to demonstrate a connection to a quote, reiterating again the need to discuss the quote using one or more academic vocabulary words the class has recently learned. A student offers a quote from the Douglass (2014) text, and the teacher lets it sit for a minute, encouraging students to review their own evidence selections for connections or clarification. "Listening to that quote," she says, "what key concept comes to mind? What does the quote clearly support?" When students hesitate, she asks one of them to summarize the portion of the text in which the quote came from. She then asks students to make an affective evaluation, linking the quote to academic vocabulary words that exemplify feelings and emotion (for example, suffering, disbelief). "I want you to think of the word that best captures the situation," she says, giving students a minute to reread and analyze. One student volunteers *desperate*, but others verbally disagree. "Do you think *desperate* describes the narrator's state of being?" she asks the class. Several students respond, some sharing quotes that confirm and some that reject.

"We have some conflicting ideas here," the teacher says, "but we haven't addressed our problem yet." She asks the students to find someone they may have disagreed with and, making sure to include both texts, take two or three minutes to discuss what they're thinking about what the texts say about the human condition. Moving about the room as they do, she selects the most provocative idea she overhears—that *maybe no one is free*—and has the partner of the person who said it share it with the class. The group then discusses, with the teacher soliciting ideas from those who agree and disagree while citing evidence. After roughly seven minutes on that idea, she expands the conversation. "Who had another idea about what the texts say about the human condition?" She again has students respond to the idea and discuss evidence in support of or refuting the idea. With the end of the period approaching, she asks students to return to their desks and adjusts their exit tickets to accommodate the discussion. She tells them, "Pick one of the two claims you heard today and discuss how *Chains* extends or refutes this idea."

This chapter focuses on the power—not just role—of talk in ambitious instruction. Recall how one important principle of ambitious instruction (see the introduction, page 1) is teachers supporting student thinking *during* learning. The success of the inquiry model I describe in chapter 3 (page 69) depends on the teachers' ability to elicit and press students' thinking in order to help them understand key ideas and participate fully in inquiry (Saye, 2017). Indeed, intentional and structured opportunities that the teacher creates and facilitates have a specific term in this chapter: dialogic inquiry. As the name suggests, *dialogic inquiry* privileges collaboration and discussion—between teacher and student and among students—as the means of pursuing answers or solutions to the guiding problem. You saw as much in the inquiry model presented in chapter 3, where every single one of the features of ambitious instruction—task potential, task access, inquiry space, multi-text integration, and interactive argumentation—depends on the ability to facilitate in the moment and sustain energy and enablement in meaningful intellectual work. The pedagogical implications of teaching students to do this kind of intellectual work as they read across sources and construct arguments are significant—you no longer guide students to answers, you guide them to *think*.

Before unpacking how to guide students to think, it's important to know what this chapter does *not* do. It does not provide talk moves—specific, individual teacher facilitation actions, such as restating, intended to increase the amount of student response and participation—nor does it explicate question types or stems; these matters are discussed in greater detail elsewhere (see, respectively, Michaels & O'Connor, 2015; Depka, 2017; Wilkinson & Hye Son, 2009). This is not to suggest there isn't guidance on how to teach ahead; there is plenty. Rather, the focus of this chapter will be on the features of productive dialogue and, primarily, its *function*—that is, why you are positioning students as dialoguers in the first place. Student thinking and learning, after all, are connected to what the teacher is asking them to do during talk; changing a few techniques won't fix fundamental issues (Boyd & Markarian, 2015).

Making Talk Rigorous

Dialogic inquiry has two major functions in an investigation: (1) to help students realize the instructional goals and solve the problem and (2) to improve the collaboration and collective problem-solving skills of students to increase their capacity in leading future dialogues. That may seem self-evident, even reductive, but consider what it implies: talk—that is, students' ideas themselves—will lead to conceptual understanding, argumentation skills, and academic rigor. This significantly ups the game for teacher design and facilitation of discussion. In this book's conception, responding to students' ideas involves more than eliciting, acknowledging, or even correcting or affirming student responses, it means facilitating students' ability to engage in disciplinary reasoning (that is, students' thinking in science). You should focus on not only asking open-ended and cognitively challenging questions but also providing feedback, connecting students' ideas, and enabling students to extensively elaborate theirs—and others'—ideas. Often referred to as responsive teaching, the hallmark of dialogic inquiry is the teacher's responsiveness to students' needs and thinking—*during* and *through* their thinking.

A substantial body of research supports the notion that giving primacy to student thinking in the planning and facilitation of instruction improves the quality of both teaching and learning (National Research Council, 2012; Windschitl et al., 2011). This is because when teachers adopt a listener stance, noticing and attending fully to how the topic or concepts students are learning make sense to them, they can do a number of pedagogically productive things. They can make ideas visible, draw connections between ideas and the discipline, engage students in sense making around their thinking, and so on (Reznitskaya, 2012). This is teacher facilitation that focuses on the substance of students' ideas, rather than on merely judging or fixing them. It is teacher facilitation that positions and encourages students to make their stances on problems public, ask questions, and present lengthy, elaborate explanations of their ways of thinking.

Of course, this type of teaching, in which you interpret and assesses students' reasoning in the moment, requires you to be highly adaptive. You cannot simply predetermine what will happen in the classroom and then try to direct students toward it. Instead, to adopt this style of teaching, you should concentrate on the following ideas.

- **Create discussion spaces that are dialogic, collaborative, and supportive:** You position discussion as a space for a class to come to agreement on the most reasonable answer or solution to the problem; you encourage conflicting voices, and if students propose multiple potential solutions or answers, the class works to understand points of disagreement and codify criteria to appropriately asses the best ideas. You support this co-construction of ideas by helping students connect ideas to the goal or problem underlying the investigation.

- **Share ownership of the dialogue with students:** This includes both the product and process of student involvement. Students' ideas about texts or problems are as equally relevant as yours. Students are also leaders in discussion by managing turns or sharing processes, asking questions, responding to each other's ideas, and so on.

- **Use facilitation moves intentionally:** Your goal is to enable extended periods of student-to-student or student-led talk and to improve participation in and uptake of meaning making. This can include probing or pressing on students' ideas or reasoning, inviting students to comment on one another's ideas, or connecting or critiquing students' ideas in order to invite additional contributions (Dyer & Sherin, 2016).

Effective dialogic inquiry is also *selective*—you must consciously select aspects of student thinking that are most generative to completing the investigation and present readiness of student thinking. That means that you need to not only be able to judge whether students' answers are right or wrong but also notice how the ideas expressed by students do and do not foster understanding (Talanquer, Bolger, & Tomanek, 2015). This attention to the *germ* of student thinking, and to germinating it with and for other students, distinguishes the dialogic inquiry approach from common forms of teacher-student interaction—such as the show-and-tell approach or funneling students toward correct answers—which tend to prioritize surface features (for example, correctness) and participation rather than using discourse to improve student understanding.

That dialogic inquiry is selective also means that you need to be selective about its use, drawing from different kinds of discourse in your classroom depending on instructional goals; this may even include recitation. The instructional goal and the problem dictate the design of discourse. Dialogic inquiry may not always be the most relevant or effective method. But in support of building an inquiry space, it is often the best.

For obvious reasons, dialogic inquiry puts new kinds of demands on both you and the students, including new roles, responsibilities, and relationships. Dialogic inquiry can be difficult for both parties to enact (Hammer et al., 2012; Lineback, 2012). The demands on you are legion. Next-level capacity to be present in order to anticipate, listen to, and sequence the substance of students' ideas are all necessary. The ability to unpack the substance of that thinking in ways that make it accessible to your students in a class and the establishment of a learning environment where ideas are freely exchanged and differences are respected is critical. No easy task for even the most experienced teacher.

The big takeaway is that innovative forms of teaching are only as good as the extent to which learners are positioned to participate in them. We can construct the most thoughtful problems, design the most engaging learning sequences, create the most meaningful culminating assessments—but all of this is for naught if students can't access the content during instruction. Such support extends beyond the designing and sequencing investigations with high-cognitive demand, *task potential*. It requires careful attention to how we maintain the integrity of the task and ensure student work is up to standard, too—*task implementation*. Take another look at the inquiry model presented in chapter 3 (page 69), and you can see multiple opportunities for realizing task implementation.

- Teacher-student or student-student discussions are key learning experiences throughout an investigation, designed to foster or facilitate student reasoning.

- Students' ideas are the center of discourse, their ideas taken up regularly to advance learning; students respond directly to one another, both during discussions and in subsequent activities.

- Talk is scaffolded: it's timed and sequenced to maximize sharing and listening, and to support further understanding of the problem.

So far, I have set you up to facilitate the investigation, but there is still the question of the facilitation itself.

Guiding Students to Synthesis

You may have heard it said that writing about music is akin to dancing about architecture (Mull, 1979). Writing about how to respond to students in the moment feels equally futile and difficult. This section, as I noted earlier in the chapter, will not cover all the components of facilitating student discussion (for example, what types of questions to ask). In fact, quite deliberately, I do not address most components of discussion. Instead, the focus will be on positioning and promoting student responses to achieve our function, or purpose: to help students generate new knowledge through integration of and connections across the texts—that is, synthesis. The processing and problematizing I describe in the pages that follow can take many forms—evaluative, causal, comparative, and alternative solutions or explanations—and can occur at multiple points during the investigation. They're always available to the teacher to leverage.

Given the impossibility of covering all the ways students—or teachers—could respond in the back and forth of classroom discourse, the focus in the following two subsections will be on techniques you can and should plan for in advance of instruction. They do not represent the whole of discussion, but they'll have you covered and ready to push student thinking.

Elaborative Processing

Processing here refers to using that student talk (the elaboration) to help students comprehend and connect what they're learning. Note the function: it's not just to talk more; it's talking to *understand* more. Research has shown that novices (that is, your students) who engage in multi-text inquiry often default to a problem-solving approach that relies on accumulation and sharing of facts rather than drawing out connections and integrating meanings. They cannot step up to synthesis without support (Bråten et al., 2013). You can use discourse to push the building of interrelationships among texts.

You will want to build the habits of self-monitoring and association, the former to ensure students are aware of how they are reading multiple texts, and the latter to ensure students consciously construct bridges between texts. You can use the suggestions that follow individually or in a group. They're useful throughout the investigation model, but particularly good for the connecting portion, and to help connect or summarize what students are learning in the constructing phase.

  ○ **Self-explanations:** Essentially a shared-aloud think-aloud, this is quite literally processing elaboratively—that is, pressing students to share how they made sense of content, such as by saying what they were thinking or wondering while reading the texts or responding to a task, what connections they were drawing within and across texts, where they got stuck, and so on. You can ask middle school students—or train them to ask themselves—to explain the *why* of their answers, and to identify how they're processing similarities and differences. You should press high school students to explain how they are processing the arguments or approaches to the problem or a perspective. Use one or two students' efforts at processing as a launching pad to identify opportunities and barriers within the texts to explore what they are learning, asking students to explain emerging relationships.

o **Relational reasoning:** On their own, students can identify a set of evidence in support of a problem but will likely miss how the texts relate to one another. Guidance can make evidence generative and educative when you direct students to make connections across texts. You can push students to add or generate examples to build on intertextual connections by:

- Finding examples across texts that are similar (analogy)

- Finding examples across texts that are in conflict (antithesis)

- Finding examples across texts that are unusual (anomaly)

- Finding examples outside of the texts that relate (application)

Be sure and have students step back from the specific examples to clarify or summarize how the texts relate; encourage them to code or classify the texts (again) based on their understanding. Prompt them to share what new connections or understandings they are drawing.

o **Knowledge revision:** Push students to consider what assumptions or beliefs of theirs have been tested by the readings or conversations in which they've engaged. Ask them to note the evidence that refutes or challenges their beliefs and their prior knowledge or evidence on the topic. The idea here is to welcome pre-existing theories or perspectives as a starting point and as malleable. Encourage students to identify what is adding to their understanding and how additional perspectives add to their own.

Problematizing Student Ideas

To model for students how to consider and appreciate that interpretations of problems are often complex and conflicting, you need to engage students in considering multiple perspectives and varying pieces of evidence—to "problematize" what students know and believe. The beauty of problematizing is that it engages students in comprehending and critiquing simultaneously—that is, as students are evaluating or articulating perspectives, they're also taking a wider range of ideas and viewpoints, giving them a holistic understanding of the issue or topic. That aligns with our goal of supporting conscientious pluralism. Students not only construct cogent arguments but also deeply understand the content in ways that allow them to look beyond opinion and toward finding common ground.

Here are two ways to plan for such problematizing.

1. **Evaluating student ideas:** The most obvious way of problematizing students' ideas is to lead with them. Take up one or more of students' emerging perspectives and have their classmates respond. As you saw in the opening vignette of this chapter, one easy way of doing this is opening the floor to have a student or two share their ideas on the problem, asking other students to respond to them with evidence that corroborates or contrasts with theirs. You can interject as needed to direct students back to the problem or to help summarize or clarify. Such an open approach works best when the goal is discovery and expansion of perspectives. It is particularly useful during the launching and connecting portions, when ideas are just starting to emerge and coalesce. The approach that fits best for connecting (chapter 3, page 95), where the goal is to position students to construct a precise and knowledgeable argument on their own afterward, is to deliberately select and chain a set of student responses as a means of building a conversation. The purpose of the conversation is to help students test and refine their claims and to deliberately provoke follow-up responses from other classmates. One way to achieve this purpose is by leading with a student's response that is different from or antithetical to others in the class. Alternatively, you can pick a claim or solution that is common among classmates and invite counterarguments to or critiques of it. Additional student responses should be those in which students can engage in refining the nuances and supports of the argument—useful practice for all students as they consider how to improve their own work.

2. **Testing:** Whereas typical probing of student thinking is often limited to asking students to further explain their thinking or that of another's, testing *extends* students' thinking by asking them to consider the issue from a new perspective or situation (Dyer & Sherin, 2016). Just as the previous section suggests selecting a provocative or contrarian student perspective, here you generate one or press on a student response specifically to test students' ability to adapt their own perspectives and apply criteria or theory in service of solving the problem. The goal is to complicate students' thinking, both to make them question their initial positions and also to get them to strengthen their cases by considering multiple points of view.

   To test student thinking, come to an investigation with a couple of hypothetical or alternative perspectives or claims for each whole-class discussion activity (or other critical juncture). This could be a rejection of a projected common student response or an idea that students are unlikely to suggest on their own. Put your alternative perspective out there to marinate for a few minutes. Let them consider the *why* behind your claim and where it comes from. If you have evaluation criteria or a model being applied, test it out. Students should dissect the strengths and merits of the claim and consider the conditions under which it could be true or valid; you can also encourage them to improve it, or to use it to strengthen their own claim. Get students used to the idea that a key component of developing their own ideas is assessing the value of others' ideas. As students become familiar with your approach of calling into question commonly held perspectives, begin to task them with generating their own tests for one another, such as by specifically identifying divergent viewpoints and challenging each other to defend or rebut them.

Regardless of approach—be it the two in this section, or other talk moves—the key to success is making visible not only the desired discourse behaviors but also how practicing them leads to higher levels of engagement and understanding. To do so, you should regularly talk about talking, giving explicit guidance on how students can approach the collaborative task and modeling the expected talk so students can mirror it in small groups (see previous chapter), and giving in-the-moment feedback to small groups on their application (Sewell, St. George, & Cullen, 2013; van Leeuwen & Janssen, 2019).

Practicing Student Talk in the Classroom

Here's the silver lining you've been waiting for: the more teachers and students practice centering classroom activity on inquiry, argumentation, and student-led discourse, the more likely you can sustain these elements (Iordanou & Constantinou, 2015; Murphy et al., 2018; Ryu & Sandoval, 2012). Dialogic inquiry is complex, but if you're patient—and this may be the hardest and last thing to shift in instruction—and keep at it, it can yield results.

School leaders and teacher leaders especially have an opportunity here to make this shift in their schools. The key to getting results is setting up your teacher learning so that collaboration and practice lead to improving discourse in your and your teachers' classrooms. Patience is rewarded. You do not need to dive right in to trying out dialogic inquiry, or even the components of the inquiry model. Better to spend your or your teachers' time orienting their ears and eyes to student thinking—in other words, what to listen for and how to listen.

To do so, start with what you do know: the content. Together as a group or in grade- or course-alike pairs, discuss a shared text (or a task situation that is needed of the right text), making sure all teachers are clear on what students should know and be able to do, and how students are likely to respond to the text. Develop some potential questions to ask or fix-up strategies you could employ. Task yourself or your teachers to implement this lesson or investigation in their classrooms without specific guidelines or mandates to follow—just let them see what happens when they are prepared to focus on student thinking. Debrief afterward. Ask them: "What did you notice? Where are your strengths or opportunities, and where are there growth opportunities?" Guide them to use their answers to these questions to identify learning needs around facilitating discussion. They can examine their ability to assess student reasoning and their knowledge and facility with enacting talk moves to support reasoning. Understanding of argumentation might also be a need area. Once identified, teachers can collect artifacts from their own practice—such as student work or videos of their instruction—and bring these to a discussion session, where the larger group, or pairs, can analyze them to determine strengths and weaknesses and specific learning needs. Teachers can set goals for identified need areas.

When ready to try it out, the group can begin to safely practice dialogic inquiry in two ways. First, set up small, daily opportunities to dialogue with different students, be it in small groups or in individual conferences. In these short engagements, you can practice pressing for elaborative processing and testing alternatives, focusing your energies on listening for and assessing students' ideas. You can also model for students how to engage in the practices, and give and get feedback on participating in dialogic inquiry. Second, have at least one group member make his or her practice public—whether by audio recording and transcribing, or by video recording the instruction—and discuss the level of cognitive demand evident in the interaction and how the teacher responded to and affected student thinking. Questions that you can use in conversation about shared practice include the following.

- How does the teacher encourage students' thinking and stimulate student discourse?

- What kinds of questions does the teacher ask? How does the teacher take up the students' ideas during the dialogue?

- What do you notice about the roles of the teacher and student?

- How does the teacher connect or help the students connect their ideas to the problem or the intended outcomes of the investigation?

You should seek consensus on naming the practices that support student thinking and discussing how to introduce them—or other practices that support elaborative processing—to students; teachers should also discuss what norms or ground rules they need to set to ensure effective conversation. During these conversations, practice using the discourse moves described in the previous section. Ultimately, the goal is to pilot these practices as you begin to employ the methods of ambitious instruction, particularly during the whole-class discussion portions of the inquiry model. Use whole-class discussion as a space for teachers to practice how to model for students how to elaborate on their beliefs and how to respond to one another's ideas. Push students' thinking forward using various discourse moves, and connect students' ideas to the problem and instructional goals of the investigation. Use the learning community to continue to study and refine these practices. From there, teachers can continue to work on integrating this approach into their individual planning and facilitation.

The Big Idea

This chapter focuses on exploring students' sense making and using it as a tool to support content-acquisition and problem-solving skills. Some key ideas to review and consider include the following.

- More than simply seeking to improve the quantity and quality of talk, ambitious instruction means leveraging student talk to conduct and complete perspective taking, argumentation, and problem solving.

- Prompting students to process their emerging understanding of the problem and problematize their emerging perspectives on the problem can assist them in extending and improving their problem solving.

- Teachers must be responsive to students' ideas—that is, not only make them the center of learning processes and activities but also leverage them to support individual and collective thinking.

- Improving teachers' ability to make students' ideas instructive requires careful study of what students know and where that knowledge can go—its emerging sophistication. (See the next chapter for more on how to center professional development on student thinking.)

Supporting and Sustaining Ambitious Instruction

Experience has taught me that the first priority of rigor, improving daily instruction, is often the last thing to meaningfully change (Cawn, Ikemoto, & Grossman, 2016). All the effort and resources in the world can't change the fact that the process is complex—hey, *people* are involved—and the gains are tenuous. The idea that a school can turn around and meet the needs of *all* its students in three to five years is a myth—try more like seven to ten (see Cawn et al., 2016). The improvement process never stops.

That's why, when I talk instructional change, I don't start with the dream—that is, the cool projects and all the other idealized images we get in our heads when we imagine bold initiatives—nor even the rallying cry to get started. No, I start with death: a premortem on why it will likely be difficult to move to and sustain ambitious instruction in the first place. Consider the moving parts—dozens of teachers; hundreds (if not thousands) of students; amorphous and malleable content and curriculum; and shifting demands from local, state, and national policy. It's tough to get grounded with so many variables; any one of them could overwhelm even the best of intentions. I've seen many schools make incredible gains in culture, teacher learning, learning environment, and the like—yet still not move the needle on classroom quality. It's hard. The starting point is acknowledging that.

But I've seen it done. It truly is possible. More than that, once done, the process is replicable. Feasible, even. There's a pattern to the work that's unmistakable, and while each success story speaks with its own voice, underneath that voice is a process that looks similar across time and settings. I've seen it done at urban high schools and suburban middle schools; at charter schools and parochial schools; at schools with high percentages of diverse learners; and at schools with high percentages of gifted and talented students. It works.

It's just not easy.

In this last chapter, then, I offer a beginning for how to get started on the commitment, how to define your story. I say *story* because while the journey has foundations and touchstones, it's also personal. Despite all the frameworks and models presented in this book, it's you and your school's story to tell and to create. This chapter will get you started on the journey—the steps in the process and potential learning activities for each step—but you will map the long road ahead in the doing, in the work of getting better. (For a more complete unpacking, see Cawn et al., 2016.)

The previous chapters unpacked important building blocks of ambitious instruction. This one puts the pieces together and focuses on helping you find your entry point for getting started. First up is Go Big, which describes the long game: the multiphase, multiyear journey toward instructional fidelity in every classroom, every day. For each step, you'll find an overview of the work, guidance on how to plan and prepare to execute (Plan for Action), and activities to use with and for faculty (Take It to Teachers).

But there's nothing stopping you from jumping in right away, and that's what Personalized Professional Development (page 163) is for; it offers several ways individuals can get started before, during, or even without schoolwide efforts. In addition, I've included several Quick Start inserts, which provide ways to engage in the work immediately on a smaller scale. Choose ideas from any of these sections or from all—just get going!

Go Big: A Process for Going to Scale

So far we have focused on classroom instruction; now it's time to talk about systematic school change. The process described in this section aligns with seminal research on school improvement (Cobb et al., 2018; Hiebert & Stigler, 2017). It also reflects the growing body of evidence that a critical component of enabling teachers to engage in more rigorous instructional practices is to have and to know the trajectory of that enabling and engaging—that is, being clear on how teachers would develop capacity for ambitious instruction over time so that you can coach them toward that vision (Gibbons & Cobb, 2016). Perhaps more important, though, is the backward mapping (Wiggins & McTighe, 2005) of the process that I provide from the stories and practices of schools I have observed that are really getting it done. Rigorous instruction is happening in most, if not all, of their classrooms. These schools are distinguished by efforts that attend to both disposition and practice—that is, they're not just doing a set of activities to get better, they also believe very deeply in the desire to get better. These attitudes propel their efforts and vice versa. The attitudes are imbued in all facets of the steps I describe. In fact, given the variability and fluidity you're likely to experience in the process (even within teams!), the collective orientation of the school toward improvement may be more important than any one process or activity described in the following paragraphs.

The most visible—and audible—facet of these schools is the sheer omnipresence of discourse and activity connected to rigor. In these schools, talk about ambitious instruction is constant. Teachers and administrators are regularly in each other's classrooms, studying classroom practice in their teacher learning and collaboration structures, and using summer planning and in-service professional development time to improve on their efforts. They are constantly looking at other models and artifacts (that is, assessments, curriculum materials, and their own work) to sharpen their understanding of what rigor is and how to realize it. In their conversations about planning and enacting instruction, they're explicitly and intentionally talking and designing with rigor in mind. They truly leverage the standards, their shared definition of ambitious instruction, and their understanding of their students in all facets of curriculum design—their maps, units, lesson plans, assessments, and so on. For them, what follows isn't a set of discrete phases selectively applied to teaching and learning—it's the very DNA of the school.

Quick Start
CONDUCTING A PREMORTEM

It's as bad as it sounds; visualize death before beginning. Make an honest, critical projection of what could go wrong. So that it doesn't.

Gather your brain trust—those who will lead the work, those who will provide the feedback you need—and make this thought exercise as explicit as possible: *We agree to do a schoolwide rigor initiative, to push ambitious instruction grade-, school-, or districtwide; it fails. Why?* Ask your team or your colleagues to identify the root causes behind that imagined failure. Once you have a running list of causes, break into smaller groups to sketch out the teacher, administrator, and student actions or beliefs that reflect each cause. Unpacking stakeholder behavior, not just the cause, is key. Of course, time is likely to be an impeding factor, but, from a structural perspective, it may be somewhat out of your control; your behavior and attitude about it, however, are controllable. It's important to identify behaviors and attitudes that you can influence—so that you can.

Indeed, those are the last two steps in the exercise: (1) identify causes and underlying behaviors that will be critical to the success or failure of the initiative and (2) generate potential solutions or courses of action to address them. Use this analysis and brainstorming to sculpt your plan or vision; share it with your stakeholders. Share your fears and concerns, too. Ask what others are willing to do to be successful.

Phase 1: Getting Grounded in Ambitious Instruction

The first phase is about onboarding, getting you and your people in sync with what it is you'll be learning and doing, and why. You could do these launch activities quickly—say, in a matter of three weeks—if you feel teacher capacity is relatively strong and you have existing systems and structures that ensure your teams meet regularly and productively. If consistent collective improvement efforts are new to the school, or if teachers' capacity or bandwidth is limited, it may take much longer, a couple of months, to do it right. Springtime is an ideal start time. You can lay the groundwork for the coming year and set yourself up for planning (phase 2) over the summer.

Step 1: Creating a Vision of Ambitious Instruction

Having a schoolwide vision is hardly a new concept—in fact, you or your school most likely created one years ago as part of your effort to articulate a school mission. There and then you articulated some common overarching ideal for your school, probably something that speaks to the need to reach and support all learners, the desire to create college-ready learners, the striving to create a community of learning, and so on. Everyone does this.

But the best schools I've studied, the ones that are consistently providing an exceptional education despite the aforementioned variables, go well beyond principles. They create missions. Sure, they also articulate visions that codify how curricula, tasks, and pedagogical approaches work together to support student learning. They also make it clear why that instructional vision is critical to helping students achieve success not only in the next level of schooling but also in college, careers, and beyond. I call these articulations a *vision of ambitious instruction* (Cawn et al., 2016) not only because it entails addressing instruction as part of the school's vision but also because a strong vision will reflect and extend the tenets of ambitious instruction discussed in the first chapter of this book. Visions of ambitious instruction state the kind of learning experiences students will have over their years of schooling, and they note the programming and other systems (for example, how to use instructional time) that support these learning opportunities.

I know what you're thinking: What can *another* brainstorming project, yet another piece of paper, do for me and my school? A lot, actually. Research shows that improvement to teachers' instructional practice occurs most often in schools and districts in which teachers and instructional leaders share a vision of ambitious instruction (Cobb, McClain, de Silva Lamberg, & Dean, 2003). Teachers in schools with such visions for teaching and learning are also more likely to develop or select and facilitate sophisticated learning tasks (Munter & Correnti, 2017). Schools and districts with a collective vision for high-quality teaching and learning demonstrate greater coherence across their instructional systems, in their professional development, principal support, coaching, and other areas (Cobb et al., 2018).

What's in a vision of ambitious instruction? A balance of principle and practice is in it, that's for sure. An ambitious vision is a place to connect the beliefs, models, and practices a school wants to implement schoolwide with the ideals and outcomes it seeks for all learners. The vision might include some of the usual ed-speak—*student-centered*, *personalized learning*, and so on—but explanation of how these concepts manifest in everyday practice is also necessary. The vision might come through in the school's literacy model, how the school takes up interdisciplinary learning, the role of writing across the curriculum, and so forth. It's *aspirational*; it's what you, your teachers, and the school as a whole are working toward; and it's the direction you're going. As you do the work, the vision will also serve as the common language for learning and talking about high-quality teaching.

There is no template or format for what a vision statement looks like, and it's not the sort of thing that should have one. As the examples in the feature box suggest, vision statements can be narrative or descriptive; philosophical and high-minded; or concrete and pedagogically specific. They can be all-school or grade- or content-specific. Whatever your style, the key here is that your vision clearly conveys what you think should happen between teachers and students in order to achieve intended learning goals. The vision requires the kind of envisioning that sees students as sense makers, and that demands high-cognitive and conceptual understanding in learning activities and the core pedagogies and instructional models that support these activities.

SAMPLE VISIONS OF AMBITIOUS INSTRUCTION

- By the end of kindergarten, our students will be seen in the corner of the library, huddled over a book, reading quietly together. One student is expressing his curiosity, wondering why a shark has six layers of teeth, and his friend is sharing her favorite part from the book she read last night. Later in the day, a student shares his nonfiction story all about sharks . . .

- Questioning is central to intellectual pursuits. Teachers plan lessons that employ open-ended questions to spark discussions. In our classrooms today, the intent is for students to think critically, address ambiguity, analyze multiple possibilities, and communicate among themselves with clarity, confidence, and respect. As a result, students begin questioning each other's assumptions and ideas. An example is a class where students make connections to a previously read text, cite the text to defend their answers, and build on each other's thoughts and ideas.

- Constant feedback and directed, differentiated instruction are the building blocks of ensuring all our students have access to rigorous, on-grade-level learning. Every student will receive at least sixty minutes of small group support every day, and each will confer individually with teachers at least three times a week. Adaptive educational technology will be integrated into core instruction to provide just-in-time remediation and acceleration.

Plan for Action

Visions, not surprisingly, tend to be individualistic—and that's not a negative. Indeed, much of what drives teachers and principals to take on the challenge and complexity of their respective roles is the highly personal vision they have of what their classrooms and schools should and need to look like to be transformative. Honor personal visions, I say. Begin with them. If you're the one initiating or leading the process, lead with *your* vision. I don't mean to suggest collective envisioning isn't important; it is. But I've found that leaning too heavily on consensus building at the outset lends itself to easy verbiage and truisms (for example, *student-centered*) that don't necessarily translate into an actionable guiding document. Better, I say, to do one of the following two options: (1) create a working draft that others can assess, adapt, and adopt or (2) have all members of a cohort—say, a leadership team or collaborative team—create their own drafts and then review together, identifying convergences and divergences.

For either approach, I'd draft a one- to two-page statement that is organized around the tenets of ambitious instruction (see previous chapters) as criteria to guide both the drafting and the review and discussion of the vision. A common way of organizing the statement is by articulating answers to the following questions.

- What is ambitious learning for the grade, subject, course, and so on?

- What curricular, pedagogical, and programmatic elements address this idea of ambitious learning?

- How will we know our teaching and learning are ambitious?

Some schools also like to include a more general section on shared, cross-classroom and cross-curricular elements that answers the question, How does learning best occur every day? Figure 5.1 shows an example of a vision that a sixth-grade team might devise.

For us to realize our goals, we will be focused on four core components of a strong instructional program.

1. **Standards-based:** Every piece of the sixth-grade instructional design will be linked to the Common Core State Standards. The sixth-grade team will backward plan from these standards by creating visions, pacing guides, and daily lesson plans with aligned weekly assessments. These documents will guide our instruction and ensure that our students master the standards to the highest degree of rigor.

2. **Data-driven:** The sixth-grade team will use data on a daily, biweekly, and cyclical basis to inform instruction. Daily, teachers will use exit slips to monitor student progress and determine mastery of objectives. If students have not mastered the objective, they will be retaught later that day. Biweekly, teachers will give summative assessments to assess students' mastery of the weekly standards.

3. **Culturally relevant and responsive:** The sixth-grade team will incorporate the emotional, social, cognitive, and cultural experiences of our students into the teaching and learning process. We honor our students' social-emotional needs by providing a daily block focused on self- and social awareness and relationship management during morning meeting and mindfulness.

4. **Cross-curricular:** Sixth-grade students make connections across different areas of curriculum. They use graphic organizers and note-taking tools flexibly and across texts and genres. They engage in problem-solving strategies within and across subjects. When engaging in performance assessments, they do a range of literate practices regardless of the genre, such as summarizing the main ideas and arguments of the texts; constructing knowledgeable claims; and editing for punctuation, spelling, and grammatical errors.

Figure 5.1: Example of a grade-level vision of ambitious instruction.

By design, the initial draft of the vision should be rough; stakeholder input will help tighten it. But get your ideas on paper first. Need more guidance on drafting the vision statement? Check figure 5.2 (page 132), where you'll find a step-by-step process for how to generate the statement.

Take It to Teachers

Now it's time to launch your initial vision with teachers. At this stage, you'll want to consider the scale of the end products. Do you want a singular vision for all classrooms and teachers, or do you want teachers to leverage the initial vision to create statements for each subject area, grade, and course? The answer to this question will determine the focus of subsequent uptake.

Professional Development Activity	Goal or Outcome
Review and discuss a professional reading on ambitious instruction. Some recommended options: • Chapters 1–3 of this book • "Making Project-Based Learning Actionable With Ambitious Instruction" (Stroupe, DeBarger, & Warner, 2017) • *The Ambitious Elementary School* (Hassrick, Raudenbush, & Rosen, 2017) • *Systems for Instructional Improvement* (Cobb et al., 2018)	Generate a list of ideas and practices for your definition of ambitious instruction.
Review examples of visions of ambitious instruction.	Refine your list; determine a format and style for articulating the vision.
Craft vision of ambitious instruction.	Create working draft; share with colleagues and staff for feedback and clarity.
Determine whether to create subject-, course-, or grade-specific visions; refine the vision to pertain to each.	Have colleagues and staff identify instructional and professional goals based on the visions.

Figure 5.2: A process for generating a vision of ambitious instruction.

Quick Start

CREATING A VISION OF AMBITIOUS INSTRUCTION

I recommend a collaborative and inquiry-based approach to the work, such as the process in figure 5.2. If you and your team have not spent time aligning common language for good instruction—say, studying or using your state or district's instructional framework—it will benefit you to engage in some shared study of research on ambitious instruction and efforts to create these visions. I share some examples in the figure.

Step 2: Creating Urgency

Making your vision (of ambitious instruction) a reality starts with real talk. What is it going to take for everyone in the building—every team, every teacher—to have rich, meaningful, impactful instructional conversations about improving their practice? Making the work *work* is not just about content, it's also about culture and systems and structures—*people* work, in other words. Because so much of the work ahead will be based on collaboration and collective improvement, the relational element of the improvement process is crucial—so crucial, in fact, that you have to plan for it, address it directly before the work begins, and embed it into all facets of the work. For rigor to be realized schoolwide everyone must *believe* in the goal. This doesn't just happen; it requires intention. People work requires work.

I know; you know. But as I write this I have just returned from a K–8 school in Chicago that appears to be conjuring magic. In classroom after classroom, I observed small-group instructional time where *all* students were on task and engaged, and where the teacher was able to provide differentiated support to ensure all students could realize the day's learning targets. The tasks and texts were, I assure you, little different than what you may currently use in your classrooms (nearly everything came from EngageNY or was purchased); the pedagogies were the same, too. Something else is in play, something that may not be immediately visible in the classroom. Look closely enough, and it becomes clear: the school is committed to ensuring all students are reading at grade level, and is willing to do anything—for example, change its curriculum and pacing or provide additional targeted support to those falling behind—to ensure this happens. Teachers meet multiple times a week to monitor the curriculum and student learning to make good on that promise.

They sweat the details—all of them.

Focus and vigilance propel the work forward. You'll need to get your people on board with the vision and excited about working together. Your people will need to have a clear idea—or contribute them—to what it will entail to create and realize the vision, and what the expectations and responsibilities will be over time on the journey toward doing so. It's a plan, sure, but it's also about the agreement and commitment to work toward the goal.

Plan for Action

Schoolwide focus and commitment take time to build and sustain, but you can start with yourself. You can also use your initial vision to begin schoolwide conversations.

The conversation should start here, with the premortem: What do you project, or fear, will be the major impediment to doing this work? Typically, when I ask principals this at the outset of the process, I hear the usual concerns about teachers' content and pedagogical knowledge—truly valid concerns, of course, but hardly constructive, and even harder to fix immediately and significantly given limited professional development time and budgets. Too often the answers are outside the locus of control of the decision maker, resulting in either actions that fail to attend to root problems, or no action at all.

What I've noticed about principals who act effectively—or, at least, have a good plan toward such acts—is that they're asking themselves a different question when thinking about how to make their vision a reality across the school. The question they ask regularly is, What needs to happen—and what barriers need to be removed—in order for everyone to participate in realizing this vision? Most times, the answers are obvious and practical, for example, more time for professional development or changes to the daily schedule—structural shifts that can make a difference in how professionals engage in their work and with others. A principal at a middle school in New York City reorganized the school day so his ELA teachers spent a majority of their teaching time working with small groups and individual students. He also built in reteaching time so his teachers could address individual student needs more regularly. This is just one example.

If you start the planning process with considering how best to support and sustain schoolwide buy-in for ambitious instruction, it ensures almost anything and everything that can be changed is at least considered. The following questions address areas to audit or assess.

- Who should be involved in this work at first versus later? What are the expectations for each (and all)?

- What is the readiness level of each teacher, and who can be leveraged to support those who are not yet ready?

- Who is collaborating, and how are they—or how should they be—collaborating?

- What supports do teachers need to engage and sustain this work?

I provide this list not because all need to be addressed but because reflecting on and discussing focus areas is the best way to consider the opportunities and challenges ahead. I'd generate a list of possible answers or actions to these questions and then winnow them down to the handful that the team agrees are major levers or barriers to your goals. You could also engage more broadly in the following questions. What's it going to take? What do we need? What's standing in our way? Focus, too, on beliefs. What do teachers believe about enacting rigorous instruction, and what do we need to do to help ensure buy-in? The goal is to identify the solution space—where plans and actions may eventually live—and not necessarily the specific solutions themselves; those will come. Next, assess your initial hypotheses. Talk to your teachers to get a sense of how they feel about your target or instructional challenges, and observe their classrooms or study artifacts from the classroom. Is there evidence or agreement that the proposed targeted areas are problematic and fixable? For now, you need only seek agreement so more specific brainstorming and planning can commence.

A principal at a high school in Chicago identified her obstacle as the way teachers were collaborating in departments, which was impeding rich conversations about instruction. Her instructional leadership team (ILT) wondered if the traditional subject-area department design, a staple of high schools for more than a century, might be a barrier. Discussion with and observation of departments confirmed concerns. Departmental time wasn't being used well, and department chairs didn't have the bandwidth or capacity to lead collaborative inquiry at the level desired. Sensing an opportunity, and with teachers open to a switch, the principal took the radical step of abolishing subject-area departments, changing the teacher professional learning structure of her school to multidisciplinary learning communities organized around shared problems of practice.

Take It to Teachers

To start thinking about how to build and sustain buy-in, I'd plan intentionally on how to ask your staff or colleagues the same questions listed in the previous section. Here are two approaches for how to do the people work.

One approach is to focus more broadly on your team and the school's beliefs and present readiness and less, for the moment, on the vision you've constructed. Frame the session as an initial calibration toward future bold moves, that as a school faculty you want to know what is necessary to take the next step. In small groups, teachers can discuss the same questions noted previously. What's it going to take? What do we need? What's standing in our way? Solicit input on what faculty would like to see in the vision statement. Note how future work will involve this vision and studying your own and your colleagues' practice.

Alternatively, another launch approach is to share the tenets of ambitious instruction or the initial vision statement you drafted. If you're not quite ready for or interested in codifying a vision, you can also share excerpts from earlier chapters on ambitious instruction. Your goal here is to get initial agreement on the principles—in other words, to establish some baseline consensus about what you'll collectively discuss and do moving forward. Read and discuss the statement together. See what the staff is excited about, as well as what they fear. Ask what they are willing to change to achieve their goals. Solicit feedback on how to expand and refine the initial statements (or the applications of ideas here). Agree on how everyone will contribute to solidifying the vision. Will they write their own drafts? Expand a collective one? Simply agree to adopt or adhere? Whatever the case, be sure to discuss how to integrate the vision into collaboration norms, and solicit input on other areas in which you could integrate the vision—future professional development, for instance, or observation tools.

Now, let's get to work.

Step 3: Creating a Common Language

Belief begins the process while knowledge propels it. In order to make rigor matter, in order to inspire change not just in individual lessons but across lessons and across classrooms, rigor and ambitious instruction need to shift from an abstract concept to an operational construct that can be studied, practiced, and known. That knowing needs to be shared and understood by all, and in complementary ways. The next step, then, is to move beyond initial agreement and toward schoolwide internalization of the vision.

There are three components to collective understanding. The first is a clear idea of what terms like *ambitious instruction* and *rigor* mean, such that all teachers can and should be held accountable for enacting them. To do this, you need to make the concepts behind these terms clear and measurable. The second is a clear idea of what rigor looks like in action: rigor as a *practice*—what it is teachers and students are doing in the interaction of teaching and learning. This should be describable and visible. The third is a clear idea of what enables and impedes rigor—in other words, the *system* in place (culture, context, capital) that will affect concept and practice. The goal here is simple: build a shared knowledge base that can, as teachers move to planning and enacting, develop into shared action.

Plan for Action

As much of the suggested activities in this section leverage the criteria for ambitious instruction described earlier in this book, you'll want to reread the introduction (page 1), Delving Into the Two Tenets in chapter 1 (page 14), and Implementing Ambitious Instruction: The Fundamentals from chapter 3 (page 70), as well as consider what common definition of rigor you want to utilize in conversation with your stakeholders. Now is also a good time to revisit or revise the draft of your vision of ambitious instruction, and consider what your first moves will be once the draft is at a working level of development. You could also collect the materials for the rigor audit activity yourself to conduct an initial analysis of current practice.

I'd first engage your instructional leadership team in the kinds of ambitious instruction learning and rigor you want to, ultimately, engage all faculty in. You should also discuss what is likely to occur when you do this kind of instruction. If you haven't done so already, wrap up your vision statement with the team and get feedback. Discuss where there might be tension or challenges when faculty members work on the statement on their own. Together, review the activities in this section and develop a sequence of learning for your learning communities that will support consensus building and initial experimentation.

Most importantly, I strongly recommend that you use your definitions and visions to create an initial set of look-fors that capture what counts when it comes to the practice (implementation) of instructional rigor—your non-negotiables, if you will. These will change over time, of course, and staff should know that you won't be monitoring or assessing implementation with them anytime soon. This is just to give teachers a more concrete, more practical articulation of what the work of teaching rigorously could or should look like. You really don't need many at this stage—just enough to help teachers start to move from general principle to specific application. You can and should draw from chapters 2–4 of this book for this part of the development process.

Quick Start
ENGAGING IN COLLABORATIVE INQUIRY OF AMBITIOUS INSTRUCTION

A good place to start planning for and enacting rigor is by examining the performance tasks of major state, national, and curricular assessments, as they typically reflect and prompt full performance of multiple standards. Examples of rigorous tasks or lessons may also suffice here, but be sure they have been vetted—those that come from research projects or initiatives are far more likely to be educative than, say, something on Teachers Pay Teachers.

Spend some time with your team exploring the selected task or assessment and its implications for your work moving forward. The goal isn't to create or refine new instruction (yet); it's to better understand what it could look like, and what it will take. To do so, I recommend discussing the following questions.

- What makes this task rigorous? What would be a full and rigorous response to the task?

- How does the assessment or task set up and support learners to do rigorous work? What is missing or necessary to ensure our learners are supported?

- What would it look like to do this kind of work in our existing curriculum? What would students need?

Your goal is to leave with an understanding of what the work entails and what changes; it's a pulse check, a diagnostic, a primer for future work. Keep the stakes low and the interest high.

Take the next step. You and your colleagues complete the performance task. Engage in the metacognitive act of unpacking what you did to solve the problem and respond to the intellectual demands of the task. Discuss the implications of your problem solving for what your learners will likely experience and need. Agree on the teaching points necessary to integrate tasks or assessments into your curricula.

Take It to Teachers

The two following approaches address two goals: (1) to build and share understanding on rigor and ambitious instruction and (2) to apply that framework to current practice in order to build interest in and clarity around future work to enact ambitious instruction.

1. **Concept consensus:** Build comprehension and agreement on the meaning of rigor by sharing with teachers the definition of ambitious instruction from the introduction, a working draft of your vision of ambitious instruction (if you haven't already), and the look-fors that I mentioned in the previous section. Start by making sure all agree with the general definition of ambitious instruction. Next, discuss how it is—or could be— integrated into the vision or look-fors, taking suggestions or adaptations to improve the documentation. Provide participants an opportunity to self-assess the degree to which their current practice aligns with the articulations and to identify potential target areas for the whole school and individual teams to address.

2. **Rigor slice:** Schools often conduct a schoolwide learning walk as a diagnostic of the current state of instruction, but I find brief classroom drop-ins to deduce problems that are likely already known often fail to maximize the power of a schoolwide study of practice. It's far better to have open conversations sooner rather than later and save classroom visits for when the goal is to clarify or assess potential solutions.

   An alternative approach I find more informative at this stage is to examine a day in the life of teaching and learning at the school by collecting a "slice" of classroom tasks and student work in a specific content area, grade or student type, skill or performance, and so on. The purpose is simple. We want to take a snapshot of what schooling looks like on, say, any given Tuesday, and see how it lines up to the conceptualization of rigor we're learning about, both in terms of what we're doing pedagogically and how students are performing the task. We also want to build urgency without putting pressure on or singling out teachers. Our goal and task are the same and twofold.

   a. By looking across a sample of classroom tasks, we can ask, "What are students actually being asked to do, and is it really intellectually rich?"

   b. By looking across samples of student work we can ask, "What sort of work are students actually producing, and is it really intellectually rich?"

Inquiring into such questions gives us a collective assessment—a progress check—on the cumulative intellectual work of the school, both from teachers and students. It also provides a chance to refine and expand the schoolwide definition of rigor and ambitious instruction, integrating elements already present in instruction and including elements missed.

Directions for the activity appear in figure 5.3. I recommend doing this activity twice: first with your brain trust—say, an ILT or other teacher leaders—so you can develop a consensus snapshot of the school writ large; and then with all or many faculty to get a sense of teachers' perceptions and needs.

Before facilitating the activity, you'll need to collect the tasks of every single classroom in a subject area (or across all of them) on a single day or over a multiday period (for example, a week).

1. Participants first review your vision of ambitious instruction and look-fors; the group reaches consensus on what criteria or descriptors to prioritize when reviewing tasks.

    a. **Round 1:** Form groups by grade, course, or subject area, and have each group review only their tasks, identifying patterns or trends in the identified focus areas. Share.

    b. **Round 2:** Mix up the tasks and groups so they contain examples and teachers from each grade, course, or subject area; redistribute to each group, and repeat the activity.

2. Discuss trends (for example, what strengths, challenges, and opportunities do you observe?) and implications (for example, what does this tell us about what work we need to do?) of findings across groups.

3. Determine next steps for school, departments or grades, and individual teachers.

4. Revisit your vision and look-fors, and revise as needed.

Figure 5.3: Directions for facilitating a rigor slice.

As you can see from the way the rigor slice culminates, one key desired outcome of the activity is more desired outcomes—more subsequent effort among cohorts to continue to assess and make sense of where teachers are, more learning demands to help better understand the work, more tweaking of the vision, and so on. The goal here is not for teachers to change their practice; it's for them to better understand why a change in practice may be necessary and what that change entails.

Step 4: The Quick Launch Pilot

Pilot before planning? Yes, it is possible; in fact, it is necessary. As noted in step 2, teachers need to see rigor as a *practice*—that is, the actual work of teaching and learning needs to be visible so that the performance of ambitious instruction, warts and all, is clear to those who will engage in the work. Seeing an initial attempt at an investigation will assist them in planning their own.

To get there, this step plots out a low-stakes, (relatively) easy-to-implement practice round of a sort that you and your team or colleagues can implement both before planning and as a launch *to* planning. Think of it as a two-level investigation. You and other colleagues will plan and implement a short investigation in your classrooms while other colleagues will observe and study these efforts in pursuit of answers to the following question: What does ambitious teaching and learning look like, and how should we move forward on implementing it? Treated as inquiry, the question provides not only a coherent, centralized approach to codifying ambitious instruction but also practice in implementing the inquiry model.

The focus on the level of the investigation is a deliberate attempt to find the right grain size of teaching that helps teachers zoom in on improving daily instruction while keeping it whole—that is, ensuring that the full complexity of the teacher's work can be made visible. Focusing on discrete elements, such as one component of the investigation or one teaching move, may obscure the multitude of elements that shape the efficacy of instruction. However, focusing too broadly, such as on designing several modules, will not assist teachers in homing in on how to facilitate the interaction between students and content. Working on and observing a multiday set of instruction is taxing and challenging for teachers already stressed by existing demands on their time, but it provides the clearest and most powerful launching point for getting started on the work in their own classrooms.

Plan for Action

Start by determining the structure of participation—that is, who is involved and their roles vis-à-vis your goal or purpose of building knowledge and increasing accessibility. Ideally, as many teachers as possible are involved hands-on in this initial proof of concept exercise, but the demands of the work and the readiness of participants may not make it feasible for all stakeholders to participate equally. The most inclusive approach is to have every learning community or teacher team in your school participate, with the teacher leader of each spearheading collaborative planning—either as co-creators or through feedback and support—to an investigation in one grade or course the group teaches. If time, resources, and readiness prohibit schoolwide involvement, an alternative approach is to seek transdisciplinary opportunities for collaboration—for example, ELA and science can work on topical or ethical science issues (such as climate change), or ELA and history can work on a civics issue (such as the role of technology in supporting versus impeding democracy). If this, too, is not feasible, select the teachers who are most ready, available, and interested in trying this out to be the proverbial guinea pigs. You can also consider having a science teacher try it out, as it is the subject where inquiry is most embedded and explicit in curriculum and instruction. Science teachers could adapt a minilab to fit the investigations model, including adding more written texts—that is, beyond simply the data students collect and the procedure they may review or follow—and writing.

Once you have a clear idea of the design of the pilot, take that plan to your ILT or leadership team, letting your team members know the plans to conduct an investigation on investigations. Now is a good time to review chapter 3 (page 69) with the team if you haven't already. Introduce the problem—feel free to adjust—and return to or create your look-fors to discuss initial impressions about what you expect. Review your vision and plans to study this question, either by talking through what you had in mind or by reading and discussing the steps described in this section. Work to build consensus on process: who will be involved and how; how the investigation will be designed, and the time and structures needed to build it; and the role of the team in supporting the work. Additionally, you'll want to discuss how the team will monitor the implementation of the pilot, using activities to create a project sequence and plan—for instance, you'll want to set aside time for the team to review and give feedback on the planned investigations, to learn the piloting procedures, and to analyze and debrief the findings. See table 5.1 for potential leadership team supporting activities. Figure four to six weeks to complete planning, execution, and evaluation of the investigation.

Table 5.1: Summary of Quick Launch Pilot Process

Steps	Teacher Team Activities	Possible Supporting or Supplemental Leadership Team Activities
Introduction	Introduce pilot goals and process; review the investigation model and criteria or look-fors.	Develop implementation steps and collaboration procedures.
Planning	Create or review investigation; anticipate student thinking.	Review the drafts of investigations and provide feedback; identify opportunities, challenges, and needs for future planning based on them.
Observation	Review observation process; conduct observation.	Facilitate observations; monitor and aggregate data collection.
Analysis	Debrief observation; discuss planning and next steps.	Analyze aggregate data and teacher planning needs; determine next steps.

(Note: If the investigation model in chapter 3 [page 69] seems too ambitious for you and your school, feel free to adapt the following activity to a single or a few lessons. To do so, use the vision and look-fors you've created to have leadership team members adapt or design a future lesson; you can use the same inquiry process, just with the single lesson.)

Take It to Teachers

The professional development model described here draws from a mix of lesson study, learning walk, and research methods. That's by design. You're aiming for collaborative inquiry that feels both educative and purpose driven. Set the tone by angling it as such. Let your people know that they're learners, but you're also building toward meaningful change to future instruction. See how they want to do this.

As you review the procedures, here is a seemingly counterintuitive recommendation to keep in mind: resist the urge to provide significant support or scaffolding to teachers—especially struggling ones—throughout this process. Know that the planning and performances are supposed to be messy; they may even be terrible. Rather than trying to play catch-up or hype the work, both of which may create unnecessary anxiety and resistance, give your teachers space to make sense of existing and future instruction through the work. You should accept and discuss confusion and even resistance. I've tried to provide some flexibility in activities, too, so you can adjust the process based on your and your team's interests and schedules.

Table 5.1 (page 141) summarizes the process, including how the leadership team can offer support. More detailed descriptions of each step follow.

Introduction

The purpose here is to introduce the inquiry project and frame the work ahead. Articulate the goals of the project and the guiding question. Explain how the work will unfold and teachers' roles. (You can also solicit their input or interest in participating further.) If you have not done so already, introduce your vision and look-fors of ambitious instruction to teachers. You can also review relevant excerpts from this book. Using artifacts from current or recent instruction, have teachers review and discuss how the tenets or criteria of the newly developed vision live or don't live in their practice. If you're having teachers participate in designing the investigation, have them read chapter 3 (page 69) for the next meeting. This part should take about forty-five to sixty minutes.

Planning

Here you'll set up teachers to participate in preparing the investigation. If teachers are not already familiar with it, review the components of the investigation model before jumping into planning.

If the teachers are planning the investigation together, start by reviewing the existing lesson or unit the classroom teacher intends to modify to fit the investigation model, at the very least skimming the texts and tasks together to get a feel for what students will be engaging. If you will use entirely new content, start by having the teacher verbalize his or her vision and goals for the investigation. Once everybody is clear on context, review the grade and subject standards, and determine relevant grade-appropriate learning benchmarks. Adjust goals as necessary to ensure alignment to standards. Use the goals to create or modify the problem guiding the investigation—review chapter 1 (page 13) as needed—and determine the logical culminating product for the investigation. If you have identified texts, review them to assess alignment with the problem and assessment. If you will require new texts, identify their function to the investigation, and search for texts that match, using the text's purpose for solving the problem to sequence its use and the appropriate methods to support it. Continue to add to the model by determining what to model, identifying questions and discussion opportunities that can support and scaffold student understanding, and so forth. If not yet determined, choose who will be piloting in his or her classroom.

If the teachers are reviewing an already-created investigation, frame the goals for the investigation and review the problem. Teachers should then review the plans for the investigation against these components and the vision and look-fors, assessing whether the planned instruction aligns with and is likely to achieve the goals and criteria. Discuss the feedback as a group, identifying opportunities to improve alignment to the frameworks.

Regardless of the approach, finish up the process by predicting how students are likely to engage or respond to each component, identifying both likely misconceptions and opportunities for divergent or alternative thinking. Agree to possible new approaches should opportunities arise. (This part should take about sixty to seventy-five minutes if reviewing an investigation. It will be more like two to two-and-a-half hours, including out-of-team planning time, to create one.)

Observation

The observation process is a little more involved and idiosyncratic than teachers familiar with peer observation are used to. Start by explaining to teachers that you'll be studying teaching through student engagement and thinking, not just observing teacher moves. The purpose of this is to see how students experience inquiry so we know to build upon it when we take it back to our own classrooms. Acknowledge the pilot teacher for taking on the role of the group guinea pig. Note how everyone else will be serving in a dual role as participants and as the pilot teacher's eyes and ears—rather than assessing the quality of the lesson—when it comes to how students respond to and approach the given tasks.

Break down the observation process. Explain that each member of the team will sit with a different pair or small group of students and observe how they respond to the components of the investigation. Distribute or have teachers create a four-column note taker. The first column should identify the investigation component under study (for example, launch, positioning). The second should list the activity or task students are assigned to complete (such as to develop an initial claim in response to the problem or to read and summarize two excerpts). The third should be where the teacher can record student thinking and problem-solving strategies. The fourth should be for additional observation notes, such as student learning challenges, engagement or focus on task, teacher intervention, and so on. (I would recommend creating these notes on a shared electronic document, such as a Google Doc, so that teachers can see all observations.) Teachers will complete the organizer by observing students in their groups and recording their findings. Let them know that it is okay to participate as a learner or teacher in the group—such as by probing students' thinking or directing them to evidence in the text that might support their under-standing—but just make note of where teachers supported student learning.

Be sure and have one person—or the pilot teacher him- or herself—record video of the classroom for the debrief. (This part should take thirty to forty-five minutes, plus classroom observation time.)

Analysis

Start the debrief by reminding the group of the problem guiding the investiga-tion. Feel free to do a quick poll to see if teachers feel they have a clearer idea of the content and process of an investigation. Select portions of the investigation to study later in the debrief by asking teachers to identify and share a key moment in the instruction when they had questions, wonderings, or even concerns. Determine—by yourself or as a group—which moments to zoom in on later in the session.

Begin the analysis by tasking the team to review the observation data they collected—either as a shared electronic document, or with copies of everyone's note takers in hand—and discuss trends in what they saw. Be sure and press teachers to point to evidence in the notes to support their claims. Continue to discuss how the data aligned with or deviated from individual observations until the group has identi-fied and agreed to a set of analyses on how students respond, good or bad, to the tasks.

Next, share with the team a subset of student responses to the culminating assessment—a random drawing of eight to twelve responses or a chosen mix of those of high, medium, and low quality—and task them to review and discuss the following.

o What patterns do you notice in terms of the type and quality of student response? To what extent do these responses realize the instructional goals of the investigation?

o What connections or relationships do you observe or hypothesize between students' written work and what we observed in classroom instruction?

o What role did the instruction play—or not play—in the resultant student work?

The goal for this discussion is to develop initial causal relationships among teacher facilitation, student collaboration, and individual performance. Identifying them can lead to clarity or direction on potential trouble spots, student learning needs and teaching points, and future work for teachers—additional learning or adaptations to the model—before group members implement in their own classrooms. Feel free to ask after these three things, even. Just be sure to honor what students did by discussing the emerging sophistication of their ideas—that is, where you can observe cogent and meaningful thinking, even in rough or fledgling form, in response to the problem. (More on *emerging sophistication* on page 159.)

With some shared ideas as to what happened and how to move forward, now you can focus on facilitation, looking at selected samples of the video recording of the investigation. Feel free to query the group again on particular teaching points relevant to the review conversation, or select the one or two most relevant ones based on the conversation's development. While watching, ask the team to consider how the teaching they observe reflects the claims or conclusions developed during the debrief and what they might do to improve or enhance their instruction when implementing it in the future.

When finished analyzing the classroom and teacher data, offer the pilot teacher a chance to reflect on the experience and what feedback resonated with him or her. Solicit questions for the teacher and any other aspect of the process, such as planning or aspects of the investigation model. End by reaching consensus on small-stakes next steps, such as trying out or adopting individual elements of the model, agreeing to develop or revise problems, auditing texts, and so on. (This part should take about one to two hours.)

Subsequent conversations or collaborations among teachers should center around either creating curricular products for classroom use (for example, investigations, problems, and so on) or examining what happened when they tried out the practices in their classrooms. Continue to check in on teachers to see what they need, and what they need to know, to move forward. Following implementation of the investigation inquiry, the instructional leadership team should debrief what they learned, including not only patterns in the practice of the teaching but also enablers and impeders of potential uptake of such practices in the future.

Phase 2: Building a Foundation for Ambitious Instruction

Phase 1 offers numerous opportunities for stakeholders to learn about and engage principles and practices of ambitious instruction. Now the time has come to prepare to enact it. In phase 2 you put together the building blocks—performance assessments, modules, investigations—to launch and sustain ambitious instruction classroom- and schoolwide.

Putting together coherent curriculum takes time. Moreover, you'll need to be strategic about the use of time so that curriculum and instruction are not isolated from one another. I recommend completing an initial round of step 1 (developing common performance assessments) over the summer—or during staff development time at the end of the school year or just before the start of a new one. Then engage step 2 (planning initial modules) on a quarterly basis for the subsequent school year. You can do step 3 (expanding and aligning) in the spring or summer following the school year. Schools I have worked with that have taken this gradual, across-the-school-year approach—using a combination of staff development days and teacher release time to give teachers blocks of time each quarter to collaborate—not only created manageable, non-anxiety-inducing processes but also enabled teachers to use these occasional planning sessions to review and refine enactment of previous blocks of instruction, therefore allowing more timely tweaks to subsequent instruction.

Step 1: Developing Common Performance Assessments

Performance assessments are just about the biggest bang for your buck there is when it comes to curricular overhaul, particularly at the outset of an instructional shift. They're a manageable amount of work and, when designed and implemented well, can impact subsequent curriculum design. Indeed, shared performance assessments—the *common* part denoting that multiple teachers from an entire grade or course would create and own such an assessment—can serve as anchors for both teaching and learning. They're tools to align and develop curriculum that enables rigor. They're tools to monitor students' progress in that curriculum. They're summative in terms of capturing what students know and can do but formative in their utility to improving teaching and learning (Dever & Lash, 2013; Stiggins & DuFour, 2009).

In chapter 2 (page 39), you learned that the kind of performance assessment that supports ambitious instruction is one that gives primacy to performance of multiple literacy skills (for example, writing, reading, and speaking) in response to a content-specific and argumentation-rich problem. These are also the features of several key college readiness assessments (for example, SAT, AP), not to mention postsecondary coursework. The focus in this step is on helping teachers build these assessments and embed them into the scope and sequences for their grade or course.

Plan for Action

Everything starts with the rationale for developing common performance assessments in the first place. The focus and frequency of their use follows from there. Part of the conversation you'll want to have with your colleagues is one about increasing opportunities for students to learn through and from rich tasks, but you'll also want to make the case for why performance assessments—especially ones co-created by teachers—are the right entry point for developing a rigorous core curriculum. Solicit feedback from teachers on your planned sequence of instructional product development over the next several months or year.

Once it's clear what it is teachers will be doing and why, agree on stipulations and expectations—how many performance assessments should be developed and implemented the first year, who will collaborate with whom, what criteria or requirements should be set for their design. If you're looking for a starting point, consider four assessments at the subject or course level—one per quarter, essentially. That number is likely to increase as you develop and sequence modules, but at the outset it serves a number of purposes: (1) it gives teachers an anchor for eight- to ten-week chunks of instruction, (2) it can serve as a useful interim progress-monitoring system toward course goals and state standards proficiency, and (3) it's a reasonable number to plan and enact. Note that not all assessments need to have a formal written response, but writing from and with multiple sources should be a part of every assessment—for example, students in a social studies class might turn in a summary of research reviewed for a speech, students in a science class might draft a design for an experiment they create. That said, at minimum have students compose one formal multipage, multisource argument per semester—that is, a final exam, research project, project paper, or the like.

I recommend creating an early adopter team, comprising representatives from several departments or grades in the school, to spearhead and pilot this process. Having reviewed the guidance in chapter 2 (page 39) on developing performance assessments, the team should come to consensus on the proposed training and development process described in the Take It to Teachers section (page 148) that follows this section and try out developing a performance task themselves. It may be useful to have one or all of them pilot an assessment prior to rolling it out with their colleagues. Have one or more of the teachers in this group facilitate the training design you'll see in the pages that follow, and have all participants lead or support subject- or course-specific planning time in their respective content areas.

Take It to Teachers

The process for facilitating development of performance assessments is designed to be malleable. You can choose to eliminate or expand components based on time and need. It is optional, but recommended, to do the first four steps with all teachers together, using mixed subject-area groups to facilitate cross-curricular conversations. You can break off into departments or course or grade teams thereafter.

As the components of the performance assessments themselves are described in detail in chapter 2 (page 39), this section will focus on the seven-part training design for teachers, not the assessments themselves. Return to chapter 2 as needed for review.

1. **Have teachers complete a practice synthesis task themselves:** As it may have been years since some teachers completed a formal multisource argumentation task, a good starting point is exposing everyone to the cognitive demands of the work. When launching such an activity, I usually use a sample AP English language synthesis task (visit https://bit .ly/2NXT46Y for a useful archive of AP English language and composition questions). They're usually focused on issues that are not content-area dependent, and they feature a mix of text types. Teachers should complete the essay assignment as if they are students. If you're pressed for time, you can stop the process around twenty to twenty-five minutes—just enough to give the teachers some substantive time on task. After stopping, give them a minute to review their work and take notes on what their thinking steps were to understanding the task, review and comprehend the documents, and prepare and compose a response. Form small groups with representatives from multiple content areas, having teachers share both their responses and their thinking steps. Groups should then move on to discussing what they anticipate will be challenging for students were they to do such a task themselves. Facilitators should observe and monitor groups, having one or two representatives either share with the whole group or summarize what they overheard.

2. **Review sample assessments in the grade or course:** Cross-examine multiple representations of what counts as a rigorous assessment for your grade, content area, and assessment purpose. I'd gather examples of content-area assessments and skill examples from multiple assessment types, including the following.

- Standardized tests (for example, SAT, SBAC, PARCC, or NGSS)

- Content-specific, classroom-based assessments (for example, EngageNY, Mars Math tasks, or tasks from Stanford History Education Group, n.d.)

- Additional assessments in line with the instructional model (for example, project-based learning examples from the Buck Institute or samples of writing tasks from an area college)

Together, look at this gathered set of assessments on two levels: (1) how and to what extent these assessments represent and reflect elements of rigor (for example, college readiness standards and core disciplinary concepts) and (2) how these compare to your existing assessments (and curriculum levels). Use these lines of analysis to ensure teachers understand both the core skills or knowledge foci of the assessments and the design elements of the task.

Quick Start
IDENTIFYING ESSENTIAL LEARNINGS OF THE COURSE OR GRADE

Narrowing down the critical learning outcomes of a grade or course can assist you and your teachers in constructing your performance assessments. I call these essential learnings because they are important to future academic work and include the state or national standards that guide your school or state. Determining them is not simply a matter of identifying a handful of priority standards; rather, you'll need to consider both knowledge and skills and the potential performances of the standards. For instance, nowhere do the Common Core standards in literacy for high school explicitly indicate that students will construct written arguments from not only two or more sources but also two or more genres; however, the performance assessments in the grade 9 EngageNY curriculum all require it. Thus, your essential learning may be a summary or synthesis of several key features or trends across the standards, not just a single standard.

To create essential learnings, I have teachers conduct a cross-analysis of three documents at once: (1) the standards for their content and grade, (2) the blueprints or examples of the standardized assessment (for example, SAT or SBAC) tied to their content area or grade, and (3) the major assessments or tasks of their curriculum. Looking across these documents, you should discuss the knowledge, skills, and performances that students are repeatedly called upon to know and do. Once you have named these core areas, teachers should articulate each more fully in the form of a statement capturing the specific knowledge, skills, and performance expected of students; typically, a given year will have four to seven statements. Compare the draft articulations to those in other grades or courses to ensure these articulations represent the specific demands of the learning in question.

Once you have agreed on essential learnings, teachers should start analyzing their existing curricula to assess alignment between expected outcomes and existing plans. Use this audit to identify opportunities in existing assessments, units, and lessons for further refinement and improvement—this will set you and your teachers up to apply the guidance in chapters 2–4 of this book.

3. **Review the vision of ambitious instruction (or aspects of ambitious instruction):** If a vision has been created, have the teachers reread it and discuss in small groups how it reflects and supports what they discussed when reflecting on the previous assessment activity.

4. **Go over goals and expectations for the work ahead:** Make clear the focus of the work and the end goal; provide a time line for when and how the work will be done, in terms of both the assessments and the future work connected to it.

   You can move into subject-, grade-, or course-specific groups at this point.

5. **Frame the assessment expectations:** Using what they learned from studying examples of grade- or subject-appropriate assessments as a starting point, teachers should review the description of the performance assessment development process in chapter 2 (page 39) and the appropriate learning standards for their course, subject, and grade. Once they review, task them to create initial articulations of what students should know and be able to do on each assessment. Once they have composed these learning targets for each assessment, look at the progression and assess coherence. Do the assessments build on one another in terms of what students are asked to know and be able to do, and how they do it?

6. **Formulate problems:** Review the problem types and problem-generating process in chapter 1 (page 13), and have teachers discuss examples and non-examples of each in their subject area, if not their existing curricula. Teams should then use that curricula to determine the major conceptual understanding expected of students at the time of each quarterly performance assessment. These can be added to the learning targets articulated in the previous step. Using the process articulated in chapter 1, turn these targets into problem statements (that is, questions). Groups should review one another's first attempts by assessing against the criteria listed in chapter 1 (that is, relevant, arguable, and sophisticated). Once

reviewed and revised, continue the problem-articulating process for the remaining assessments.

7. **Generate performance expectations:** As the design and implementation of the assessment is coming before teachers will be expected to build text sets and modules, you'll want to treat the initial assessment design as a module unto its own, with potentially its own text sets and other criteria. Teachers should discuss the following.

    - Task parameters (see criteria in chapter 1)

    - Number and kind of texts to be used

    - Amount of instructional time necessary to complete assessment

    - Instructional supports needed (for example, what students will need to be taught)

These criteria can be predetermined for teachers, too. If that's the case, use this step to go over these expectations and provide time and feedback for teachers to modify their initial assessment tasks to fit.

From here, teachers can build out each assessment in full, selecting content and designing instructional supports to complement. They can do this during individualized planning time or department time and space it out across weeks or months. Your assessment team should serve as thought partners and feedback providers during and after the buildout. Try to test out the assessments during development, not after—say, in a summer school class or with students one to one. Use the experience to guide modifications and revisions.

Step 2: Planning Initial Modules

Now that anchoring assessments are in place, you can begin to address the instructional component. At this point you are still gradually introducing and learning the curricular and instructional shifts presented in previous chapters, so no need to rush. All you are going to ask teachers to do is plan one module per assessment (per quarter). (If you're feeling ready to do more, don't hesitate.) The pace may appear glacial, but the intention is not. You want to give teachers the time and focus to not only modify or create curriculum but also learn from the process.

Make sure you and your people are up to speed on chapter 3 (page 69) before beginning this step.

Plan for Action

There are two ways of approaching the development of teachers' first module.

The first is to focus on the performance assessment modules themselves—that is, the three to seven days of instruction that would encompass setting up and completing the assessment. As with any other investigation, this would include reading of the texts, targeted direct instruction to support students' critical thinking and reasoning skills, and discussion activities to generate claims. It would also incorporate time for composing and performing the final work products. Such a focus tends to a likely need emerging from creating the performance assessments, a need that prompts the question, Now that we have this assessment, how do we set students up to do well on it? It just doesn't attend to the content or instruction leading up to it just yet.

The second is to hurry up and wait. Don't get started in earnest on building out modules until after you've administered the first performance assessment (Octoberish, if starting from the beginning of the school year). In this approach, you'll use the experience and outcome of implementing the performance assessment for the first time to guide how to organize the creation of future modules. To do so, you and your leadership team should collect three things: (1) a subset of student work from some or all of the performance assessment, (2) feedback or reflections from students on their experience with the assessment (can be done formally or informally), and (3) observations on teaching and learning during the process. Review the data together, and focus your discussion on both teaching and learning. To what extent did the design meet the rigor expectations and performance criteria, and to what extent did student work meet the learning targets? In what areas or ways do students appear to need support in order to be successful on subsequent cognitively demanding tasks? Use your findings to make the following two decisions: (1) whether to develop a stand-alone module in advance of the next performance assessment, or to do the performance assessment module and (2) what kind of guidance and instructional support students will need in future teaching. Repeat for each quarter.

In either case, assume it will take roughly three to five hours of planning time to build out the first module, and maybe three to four hours for each one thereafter. That is not an insignificant amount of planning or professional development time, I know, which is why I recommend providing teachers with a single, sustained block of time to put it together rather than ask them to do so piecemeal over the course of several weeks. I've had schools release a given team of teachers for a morning or afternoon to complete these modules; others that did not have the budget or access to substitute teachers used a portion of staff development days to do this work.

Take It to Teachers

Teachers should be familiar with the investigation model in chapter 3 (page 69) before beginning the planning process. While teachers can and may work individually on their modules, I strongly recommend having the whole team or department plan in the same space, the reason for which I explain in a moment.

If they're developing modules for the performance assessment, teachers should first analyze student performance on the previous performance assessment—or a similar assessment from existing or prior curricula—to identify student learning opportunities and challenges. If you work in the classroom yourself, I also recommend reviewing any notes or feedback you have on your teaching to identify the same. Having identified where their students are, they should next review their planned performance assessment to determine the following.

- How much instructional time is likely to be necessary for students to read and understand the texts, prepare a response, and share and reflect on that response?

- Given the task demands and prior student learning challenges, in what areas will students need support? What kinds of support?

- What should I start, stop, or continue doing in terms of activities and facilitation to best support student learning?

Answers to these questions should allow teachers to first create a macro-level layout of the learning sequence—that is, how many days and how much instructional time is necessary and the general order of activities—and then to start identifying specifics for each day of instruction, such as the goals and the specific activities or questions that they will address in each day.

If teachers are developing a module prior to the performance assessment, the process is similar to the one described in the previous paragraphs, but the starting point is existing or previous curricula—whichever you are using or leveraging. Review these instructional plans in relation to the planned performance assessment, and determine which content or components, if any, are most aligned to the performance assessment. You should also consider which elements of it are most readily adaptable to the investigation model format. Once you've found the components most aligned to and accessible for a module, consider the following questions.

- What is an underlying or essential problem of this content that connects to the problem guiding the assessment?

- Given the components of an investigation, what can I keep? What will need to be modified, and how? What will I need to create?

- How much instructional time is likely to be necessary for students to read and understand the texts, prepare and discuss a response, and share and reflect on that response?

- Given the task demands of the assessment and prior student learning challenges with past or similar assessments, in what areas will students need support? What kinds of support?

Answers to these questions should allow teachers to solidify the problem guiding the investigation, and then create the same macro- and micro-level sequences of the module.

Once teachers have developed a general plan for their modules, have them do a quick share of their plans in pairs—if they collaborated with another teacher on planning, each can work with someone else to review—but bring them back to a whole group to work on the positioning portion of their modules. Start by having team members share the learning needs or skill areas they identified and pick one or two to workshop together. Using the guidelines in chapter 3 (page 69), together build out the modeling or guided practice approach for the selected skills. Once you finish, discuss how teachers can apply the shared ideas and process to the skill needs they identified but did not workshop.

Provide additional time or feedback as needed for teachers to continue to work on their modules.

Step 3: Expanding and Aligning

The last stage of the initial curriculum development process is to formalize, develop, and sequence the remaining instructional components for the course or year so that students engage a curriculum that is not only ambitious but also coherent. This will likely require teachers to create new modules and assessments (expansion) or adjust or adapt existing instructional plans to support the goals and foci of the new performance assessments (alignment).

As noted earlier in the book, there's no need to turn every unit or outline into a module, nor would I expect that you would use the investigation format for every lesson or week. There is room for both the traditional approach and the one I present here, and a good part of the work in this stage is figuring out and planning an appropriate balance. I recommend that the formal, full-blown curriculum development process occurs after you have developed and delivered a few pilot modules.

Plan for Action

Given the differences in programming across content areas and grades, most likely teachers' yearlong learning sequences will not look the same. It will also most likely not be feasible to legislate the same number or order of modules across classrooms. Thus, empowering teacher leaders or department chairs to provide individual support to their colleagues is critical at this juncture. Everything you do to plan for further integration should go toward supporting their capacity to lead the work.

To do so, I recommend the same approach I highlighted in so many of the previous steps: collect multiple types of data on implementation and teacher perception, and use it to guide diagnoses and action to support schoolwide rollout. You can do so by employing one or more of the following.

○ **Monitor initial module implementation:** As with the performance assessments we looked at in the previous step, collect data on the initial implementation of an investigation—including teacher plans and student work—to assess implementation and identify opportunities and challenges.

○ **Conduct a broader audit of curriculum:** Earlier you learned about examining a slice of rigor in order to get an initial sense of the rigor level in daily instruction. Here, you could do a broader review of units in or across content areas, grades or courses, and times of the year in order to determine the alignment of existing instructional materials to the tenets of ambitious instruction. Consider the degree to which the existing curricula possess or can readily integrate key components of the vision and investigation model, such as problems, multiple texts, and interactive argumentation. This examination should clarify professional development or coaching needs moving forward.

○ **Survey teachers:** Use reflections, surveys, and focus groups to find out from teachers how well aligned to ambitious instruction they think their existing curriculum plans are, what additional work they think they'll need to do on their curriculum, and their perceptions and experiences implementing the performance assessments and investigations.

It may be useful to conduct these inquiries at the team or department level, thereby distributing the work across the instructional leadership team. Once you have done so and collected your findings, review and discuss them, identifying both team- or department-specific needs and more general trends and needs across the faculty. Each team leader should then sculpt a plan for their colleagues, drawing on both the findings and the process notes described in the next section.

Take It to Teachers

Chapter 2 (page 39) covers the process for developing modules from an overarching problem. Be sure and review prior to launching this work with teachers, as the process underlies the guidance that follows. If relevant, don't hesitate to spend time unpacking any of the data sources listed in the previous section with your teachers as a precursor to expanding the work.

Everything you do here begins with and centers on the performance assessments, so start there. If you haven't built those out yet, do so. If there are changes you want or need to make to the ones you've developed, refine those first. Once you have solidi-fied the assessments, the rest of the work is backward mapping. Teachers should take the problem guiding each assessment and unpack the content, concept, and academic reading and writing skills necessary to answer it fully. With that list, teachers should do the following.

○ Assess the degree to which existing or related curricula address these or *could* address these with revisions.

○ Generate a set of problems or questions that address the content and skills identified (they can use the guidance on problems and modules in chapter 1, page 13, and chapter 2, page 39).

Once they have addressed both parts, create an initial sequence of the problems, with the most accessible problem coming first, and subsequent problems building on initial learning and working toward the cumulative assessment. With a general order in place, determine which elements of existing curricula can apply to these problems, and what modifications are necessary. Group these components with their corresponding problem. (Again, if an existing unit or set of lessons can fulfill a problem or support students on the performance assessment, don't hesitate to include it.)

When teachers have a general layout of their modules and some ideas about how to leverage existing materials, have them generate a quick needs list. Are they missing text sets? Do they need to develop the investigations? Do they need to explore how to teach students components of argumentation or multi-text integration? Their findings should clarify their to-do list and the amount of time and support necessary. From there, they can generate individual plans of action. Be sure and direct staff or colleagues to the chapters and content in this book most relevant to those needs.

Phase 3: Getting Good

This final phase isn't so much a stage or set of steps as it is a state of being. It's the continuous improvement effort to integrate the vision into core programming schoolwide. This is fidelity work: ensuring every lesson in every classroom on every day is up to standard. It's vigilance, really.

In the spirit of that commitment, I present the next set of guidelines as a continuous rather than linear process, which you can start and sustain at any time (though most likely after you've gotten rolling on several or most of the previous steps). Apply any and all of these ideas in each component described on the next few pages—Building Student Buy-In, Learning From Student Thinking, and Learning From Practice—and feel free to adapt them as befits your school and your faculty. Integrate these ideas into repetitions or expansions of previous steps, even. Think of it as the third phase in number but the forever stage in implementation—it's where your vision and initiative will live and evolve.

More so than any previous stage, this work depends on and lives in your learning communities and your classrooms themselves. It's simple: we want to make changes to daily instruction, and the professional development mechanism closest to daily instruction—well, besides instructional coaching—is the teacher team and individual practice and reflection. Because of that proximity, learning communities, and the work teachers apply from them, need to be focused on the work of teaching and at a level of rigor commensurate with the rigor we seek in the classroom instruction itself. Teachers need to study their practice analytically and critically, working alongside one another to collaborate on difficult teaching tasks, then sharing what they learned through the process. This needs to be structured and intentional. You must pay real attention to ensuring it is intellectually demanding for teachers.

Instructional leadership also needs to demand from teachers their intellect and attention when it comes to enactment. The language, beliefs, and practices underlying the vision need to be embedded in all ways the school monitors teaching. Teachers should be observed and provided feedback on the established vision and look-fors; even peer observations and learning walks should incorporate these specific criteria. Collect data on what's being implemented, and how. All of it is in service of how you can do ambitious instruction better.

Building Student Buy-In

If teachers want curriculum and instruction to be more than something they do to students, they'll need to be transparent with their learners about why they are doing what they are doing and what students should expect to know and be able to do as a result. The promise and even practice of ambitious instruction—relevant problems, inquiry, and argumentation—alone are not sufficient motivation for students to feel engaged in and committed to rigorous learning. There must be a clear, meaningful purpose to it—and that's beyond simply pointing out the learning target or daily objective on the board. Furthermore, students need to be able to see and know how they are making progress toward outcomes or goals.

To do so, teachers should both set students up to understand the connection between the rigor of present instruction and future work *and* ensure they receive repeated opportunities to reflect upon it.

- **Purpose with practice:** As you're beginning to enact ambitious instruction, make clear to students the purpose for doing so—both your pedagogical rationale and what's in it for them. To facilitate the latter, teachers can devote some instructional time before launching into an investigation or performance assessment to examine the expectations and outcomes of doing intellectual work—for example, college and career readiness standards for their grade or school level, examples of tasks from area colleges or universities, items from college admissions tests, and more. I find it useful to pair two or more of these in order to discuss both what they'll be asked to do *and* what it looks like. Discuss how it compares to what they're doing now, and what might need to change in order to hit this benchmark. As students become more familiar with the investigation model, continue to show them examples—like tasks and student work—of what the work looks like at the next level, emphasizing particular features, such as how they should use evidence or the writing style or tone, on which subsequent learning and practice will focus.

o **Progress monitoring:** Empower students to own their growth by having them track their work on key skills and performances on ambitious instruction. Start by having students set goals for themselves related to their intellectual behavior—these can be standards based or centered on some element of the investigation model or outcomes. Then, as they complete each investigation or module, teachers can give students a few minutes to review their written efforts and feedback and record their progress. They can use a grade the teacher has given to them, grade themselves, or include no grade and just focus on their reflections. Continue to have them track their progress until they have achieved the goal. Repeat this process for a new goal or new benchmark for the particular skill or performance area.

Learning From Student Thinking

Examination of student thinking and reasoning—whether that is reading students' written work or observing students during instruction—is an integral component of nearly every previous step, and for good reason. We want to put students' ideas front and center to drive classroom inquiry, and research also shows that focusing on them is among the most effective professional development approaches there is for improving teaching (Franke, Carpenter, & Battey, 2008; Kennedy, 2016). Often mistakenly devised as a separate professional development entity or activity (for example, looking at student work), analysis of students' ideas needs to integrate into all aspects and foci of your professional development system in order to be effective. Think of understanding your learning standards via studying different representations of proficiency. Think of planning for instruction by using students' current levels of readiness and partial understandings to guide you. I note additional ways to attend to student thinking in a moment, but the principle is the same regardless of the activity design: student ideas should guide instruction and learning about instruction.

o **Focus on emerging sophistication:** Students are novice academics capable of impressive intellectual behaviors but quite new and raw when it comes to developing and articulating their ideas. I use the term *emerging sophistication* to note the potential inherent in their admittedly rough arguments. It's the kernel of a bright idea or ideas in initial or formative work that they can build on and teachers can support in subsequent instruction. To do so, gather samples of a written assessment at the end of an investigation—you can focus on a sample from one teacher team member's class, or you can draw examples from multiple classrooms and review together, looking not for errors or misconceptions but for where students are beginning to demonstrate more nuanced perspectives on the problem at hand, such as by taking an alternative position, applying criteria to evaluate other perspectives, discussing counterarguments, and so on. Together, discuss what students understand and how you can enlarge that understanding over the course of subsequent modules, setting goals or benchmarks for what the desired proficiency or understanding is for that student (or type of student) by and for the performance assessment. Identify teaching moves—such as future direct instruction in the positioning portion—that can support this growth. I recommend collecting and maintaining examples of this emerging sophistication on various tasks across the curricula, both to serve as future exemplars for students and to guide calibration among teachers when designing curricula or assessing student performance. You can also use your findings to develop a learning trajectory (see next bullet).

o **Develop a learning trajectory:** As I have noted throughout the book, having a clear idea of what a sophisticated response or solution is to the problem is critical to understanding what to teach and how to teach; devising a learning trajectory can help. Essentially a continuum that articulates the successively more sophisticated ways students could think about a topic, a learning trajectory functions as a progression of student learning and thinking that can not only distinguish proficient and fledgling understanding but also function as a road map for how students' understanding can and should change over time. It's a bit like a cross between a rubric and the essential understandings portion of a unit plan. Here's my quick and dirty way of creating one.

  • Gather relevant student work—if it's from the same instructional plans or content, great; if not, work on similar tasks will do—or brainstorm what you anticipate the range of student work could look like given the instructional goals of the investigation. Discuss what students already know and can do, and what it would mean to build on that prior knowledge during the given investigation or module.

- Examine the problem and the instructional goals, then discuss what it would mean for students to respond with sophistication—that is, what perspectives would they articulate, and what kind of skill performance would they convey? Use the student work to discuss what that sophistication might look like across various stages of proficiency.

- Create the trajectory by making the three to four key conceptual understandings or performances that you expect of students (that is, your instructional goals) the rows on a graphic organizer (see figure 5.4 for a template). The columns will be your articulations of sophistication, from least comprehensive and sophisticated to most.

- Identify activities and supports for students at each level of thinking.

Problem:				
Learning Goals or Targets:			**Standards Addressed:**	
	Developing	*Emerging*	*Sufficient*	*Comprehensive*
(Performance)				
(Performance)				
(Conceptual Understanding)				
(Conceptual Understanding)				
Recommended Student Learning or Supports				

Figure 5.4: Learning trajectory template.

*Visit **go.SolutionTree.com/instruction** for a free reproducible version of this figure.*

A rough draft is all you need to get going; you can refine it over time (especially if you intend to create a rubric out of it). In subsequent conversations and collaborations with your team, you can use the trajectory to refine instructional goals and tasks, anticipate student learning challenges, and develop appropriate scaffolds and activities to orient students to the kind of thinking you expect from them.

Learning From Practice

Make that *deliberate* practice. It's true that we learn by doing—but it's most effective when that doing is structured and intentional, and when we receive feedback on our actions throughout (Ericsson, 2004). It is those two elements that make or break the impact of teacher professional development, not the model itself. Practice doesn't and shouldn't make perfect; it should make teachers more deliberate about how they plan and perform. That requires teacher learning of the same intensity and intentionality.

The following assumes you already have structures in place to observe and study teachers' practice—classroom walks, coaching, teacher collaboration teams, and others—and that you are already engaging in the work in some capacity and with some regularity. Don't change that. This guidance is not intended to modify those systems and structures; it's meant to add focus and clarity to ensure that study of teachers' practice is focused and clear.

- **Weekly slice:** Take a cue from the NFL, of all places. Every week during the regular season, the league holds a conference call for referees and one for its competition committee—sort of like its advisory board for product quality—in which it examines six to ten examples of particular football practice or penalty (for example, what counts as a catch or roughing the passer). The goal is to calibrate and build collective understanding of what counts. Continuing the spirit of the slice activity (page 138), you can do something similar in your instructional leadership or teacher teams by examining instructional artifacts—tasks, video excerpts, student work—from across classrooms or across days on a shared instructional focus, such as particular content, particular parts of the investigation model, particular pedagogies, and so on. Take some time at the outset to identify collective needs, reaching consensus on priority focus areas, the ones that will most impact or move instruction across classrooms, and stick to these priorities. Give each at least four to six weeks of dedicated focus, working in professional readings, intentional practice, and feedback in addition to regular study of teacher practice. Don't move on until the team has a clear idea of how to move forward with the practice or focus.

○ **Active lesson study:** In the same spirit as the quick launch pilot (step 4, page 139), and for the same purpose, get teams involved in studying the whole process of developing, enacting, and reflecting on implementing ambitious instruction. As before, and as is typical of lesson study design, move through a cycle of learning, planning, enacting, and analyzing (see figure 5.5, page 165, in the next section). The difference here, as earlier, is the expectation that group members participate in the enactment of instruction. The easiest way to do so is via the same model we saw earlier: pick one pilot teacher in whose classroom the instruction will take place, and who will teach the lesson; the other teachers will sit with and engage small groups of students in the pilot teacher's class, serving as both participants and facilitators depending on student need, and capturing data on students' thinking and problem solving. You can also do this with teachers working one to one with students, or by teachers team-teaching certain components of the investigation model (that is, modeling a skill in the positioning portion)—whatever ensures multiple teachers have an opportunity to participate in trying out new content or instructional practices. Debriefs should focus on studying—via video, student work, and observation—implementation of the practice. Outcomes should focus on identifying the ways to refine and improve future practice in the area, with the team setting goals or expectations for individual uptake. You can run full cycles of this process a couple of times per quarter, building on—rather than taking away from—existing team foci.

○ **Active coaching:** The *active* component here refers to coaching actions that occur during teaching, such that the teacher being coached can become aware of and shift his or her delivery. To begin to integrate on-the-spot coaching into teacher professional development, I recommend starting with rehearsals. Rehearsals are exactly what they sound like: within their teams, teachers practice parts of the lesson as if they are delivering it to students, with teammates serving as participants or learners. One colleague or coach serves as director, providing real-time feedback—yes, even stopping the action or requesting the practicing teacher repeat a portion—to address and correct problem areas. Rehearsals are particularly effective for building competency and confidence in portions of the investigation model—say, the positioning portion—and for trying out newly developed material. The goal is for the practicing teacher and the other teachers on the team to get clarity on how best to deliver the material, and to get consensus on what to look for in each other's classrooms. This, in turn, paves the way for coaching during the actual enactment with students, as coaches and teammates can now use these look-fors and what they observe during student-to-student engagement to provide feedback to the teacher to guide subsequent activity. One benefit of the investigation model is continual movement between forms of instruction, creating multiple opportunities during the lesson for the teacher to take in and take up feedback in order to shift delivery in later parts of the investigation.

Ambitious? Check. Demanding? Yes. Precarious? Always. That's why it takes time; that's why it takes collaboration. That's why it's continuous. It takes rigor to improve teaching with and for rigor.

Admittedly, it's not always consistent: teams and people change; new initiatives and trends come and go. What enables schools to persevere—or even just get started— when enacting change is how individuals are positioned and enabled to learn and grow. That doesn't require a multistep plan or a schoolwide focus; it just requires a commitment to your learning and that of your students. There's no sense in waiting to give you and them that opportunity.

Personalized Professional Development

Rather than change course in your existing professional development systems, concentrate first on creating the space for teachers to work individually and independently on their learning needs. You can facilitate this in three ways: (1) individual goal setting, (2) time for personal projects, and (3) problems of practice groups.

Individual Goal Setting

Teachers should identify individual stretch goals for both teaching and learning that are challenging and novel—hence the *stretch*. These pursuits should focus on small, tangible wins that you can replicate and expand as you and your teachers learn more. That is, rather than moonshots—say, double-digit growth in student learning or immediate adoption of a new curriculum—set for yourself ambitious but reasonable changes in your own instruction that you want to commit to, such as integrating the use of scientific or psychological theories and frameworks into a literature study or having students lead a discussion and still meet the learning outcomes.

If you're struggling to identify a stretch goal to get you started, an obvious one, detailed in chapter 2, is the performance assessment, a substantive but manageable shift that can be a gateway for more ambitious moves to your practice. For instance, you might commit in an upcoming unit to trying out the assessment model proposed in chapter 2 (page 44) and the approach to teaching synthesis in chapter 4 (page 117) to support it, setting teacher practice goals for yourself without necessarily articulating expectations for student gains—you're learning after all. You can then use the experience to determine future teaching and learning needs or goal areas on which to follow up.

Time for Personal Projects

The internet search behemoth Google allows its employees to spend more than 20 percent of their work time—that is, one full day a week—on personal projects. Many of the most used products in the Google pantheon—including Gmail—have come out of these passion projects (McCracken, 2014). No reason why teachers, particularly in the early stages of rethinking their practice, can't do the same.

The structure for this work is simple and flexible—just make a regular chunk of professional development, planning, or team time available for teachers to pursue their own passion projects—but it does require intentionality with setup and monitoring. The obvious starting point are those stretch goals: use them to guide you and your teachers in selecting areas of improvement on which to work. Another option is to poll or brainstorm with staff about instructional need areas in the school, content area, or grade. You can then form teams around these areas of interest for follow-up work during personalized work time. Individuals or teams should identify goals—in particular, the kinds of work products they will produce—with the leader of the work tracking progress and sending updates to the administration on its status. Schedule short symposiums throughout the year for faculty to share their efforts or learning.

Problems of Practice Groups

You can reorganize teams around shared interests and inquiry, allowing for cross-grade and cross-content collaboration to occur. In such a program of collaboration, which you can run in single cycles (such as a couple of weeks) or a full semester or year, you can group teachers around your school's, department's, or team's instructional priorities, or you can position teachers to select their own groups based on interest or need.

I typically launch this approach by having teachers complete a shared KWL (know, want to know, learn) chart (Ogle, 1986). We quickly identify what we already know, spend most of our time posing questions that articulate what we want to know, and decide on which questions we can and need to answer first. As a first step or "homework," ask teachers to collect some data—perhaps student work from classroom instruction, survey results, or curriculum artifacts—and review a professional reading that addresses the question or problem.

It's only when we come back to discuss that I let folks know that we are engaging in an intentional cycle of inquiry, diagrammed in figure 5.5. Framing our efforts now as an investigation, we use the article and our data to answer or reevaluate our

Inquiry Cycle

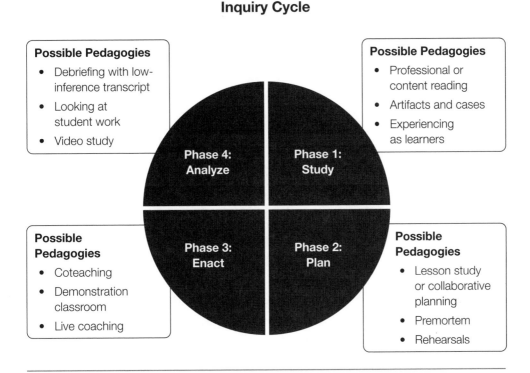

Figure 5.5: Problems of practice groups inquiry cycle.

initial questions. Our answers, in turn, become opportunities for action, and we devote time to agree on next steps and plan for implementation in our classrooms (phase 2). We schedule subsequent meetings to observe one another enact our learning (phase 3) and analyze our results (phase 4).

Note: You can use the approach in figure 5.5 for the collaborative inquiry work that we saw earlier, too.

The Big, Big Idea

Rather than summarize where we've been, let's take a breath and then think about what this all means and how it can work for you.

Teaching well is challenging; doing so across a school is complex. Success is precarious because there are threats to that success everywhere. Remember the school I mentioned that had unique vision statements for each grade? Early on in its efforts to innovate its literacy model, it let an external consultant lead a professional development session with its whole staff, all of whom had received extensive training on and had significant experience with backward design. Yet when the consultant allowed them to plan some fun activities, they immediately abandoned all that training and know-how. The administration had to step in and redirect; the professional development sequence for the week had to be revised based on the loss of focus on the real work.

I note this story not as a scare tactic but as a reminder that ambitious instruction is not natural: it requires intention and structure to create and sustain—always. Most efforts fail. Instruction of the sort envisioned in this book is rarely found or sustained in secondary schools in the United States (Greenleaf & Valencia, 2017). Having made it through the book, I know you can empathize: doing this kind of work, as you've learned, doesn't just require hard work; it requires that teachers *and* students take on roles and take risks that are new and unfamiliar to them (Beach, 2011; Porter, McMaken, Hwang, & Yang, 2011). That's hard for anyone, fully supporting teacher team (or school) or not. It requires patience, commitment, a learning orientation—all of which will be tested, maybe even for years to come.

Such focus and care begin now, even in the earliest stages of conceptualizing your improvement plans. Dream big but start personal and small. Research on goal setting in the business world (Sitkin, Miller, & Lee, 2017) has shown that organizations fail at a remarkable rate when they lack resources or commitment to full-scale change or they cobble together said resources, commitments, and buy-in—sounds like most school reforms, right? We all know how it goes: too often the curricular and instructional improvement initiatives schools set have intended goals or outcomes that aim to encompass everyone but address no one's individual readiness, needs, or interests. The result is often a set of work products or processes—unit plans, say, or new instructional strategies—without commensurate personal interest and involvement. These sorts of initiatives rarely sustain improvement; they rarely last.

Best, then, to make what matters matter—teaching and learning. The means are right before your eyes. Take the same two tenets guiding ambitious instruction—(1) problem-based learning and (2) a focus on synthesis—and leverage them to guide ambitious learning. Frame the work to your colleagues and faculty as a shared problem, one worthy of the focus of your professional development and school improvement plans. Make inquiry—through the study of practice and students noted in this chapter—the primary means by which you explore how to solve that problem, generating school- or classroom-specific practical knowledge for application within and across classrooms (that is, synthesis). Remind them that while daily instruction may be the last thing to meaningfully change, it is also the means of change—the blueprint. Learn ambitiously to teach ambitiously.

REFERENCES AND RESOURCES

Abedi, J., & Herman, J. (2010). Assessing English language learners' opportunity to learn mathematics: Issues and limitations. *Teachers College Record, 112*(3), 723–746.

ACT. (n.d.). *Writing sample essays: Essay task*. Accessed at www.act.org/content/act/en/products-and-services/the-act/test-preparation/writing-sample-essays.html on July 26, 2019.

Adichie, C. N. (2013). *Americanah: A novel*. New York: Alfred A. Knopf.

Alston, C. L., & Barker, L. M. (2014). Reading for teaching: What we notice when we look at literature. *English Journal, 103*(4), 62–67.

Anderson, L. H. (2008). *Chains*. New York: Simon & Schuster.

Anderson, L. W., & Krathwohl, D. R. (Eds.). (2001). *A taxonomy for learning, teaching, and assessing: A revision of Bloom's taxonomy of educational objectives*. New York: Longman.

Arya, D. J., Hiebert, E. H., & Pearson, P. D. (2011). The effects of syntactic and lexical complexity on the comprehension of elementary science texts. *International Electronic Journal of Elementary Education, 4*(1), 107–125.

Bain, R. B. (2012). Using disciplinary literacy to develop coherence in history teacher education: The clinical rounds project. *The History Teacher, 45*(4), 513–532.

Barringer, F. (2012, October 13). A grand experiment to rein in climate change. *New York Times*. Accessed at www.nytimes.com/2012/10/14/science/earth/in-california-a-grand-experiment-to-rein-in-climate-change.html?_r=0 on January 27, 2020.

Barzilai, S., Zohar, A. R., & Mor-Hagani, S. (2018). Promoting integration of multiple texts: A review of instructional approaches and practices. *Educational Psychology Review, 30*(3), 973–999.

Baxter Magolda, M. B. (2004). Evolution of a constructivist conceptualization of epistemological reflection. *Educational Psychologist, 39*(1), 31–42.

Belenky, M. F., Clinchy, B. M., Goldberger, N. R., & Tarule, J. M. (1997). *Women's ways of knowing: The development of self, voice, and mind*. New York: BasicBooks.

Bell, R. L., Smetana, L., & Binns, I. (2005). Simplifying inquiry instruction. *The Science Teacher, 72*(7), 30–33.

Blanchard, M. R., Southerland, S. A., Osborne, J. W., Sampson, V. D., Annetta, L. A., & Granger, E. M. (2010). Is inquiry possible in light of accountability?: A quantitative comparison of the relative effectiveness of guided inquiry and verification laboratory instruction. *Science Education, 94*(4), 577–616.

Bloom, B. S. (Ed.). (1956). *Taxonomy of educational objectives: The classification of educational goals; Handbook I: Cognitive domain.* New York: David McKay.

Bloome, D. (2015). From learning to argue to arguing to learn: Recontextualization, entextualization, and collective memory. In P. Enesco (Chair), *Literacy, Equity, Imagination (65th Annual Conference of the Literary Research Association).* Symposium conducted at the meeting of the Literacy Research Association, San Diego, CA.

Boaler, J. (2016). *Mathematical mindsets: Unleashing students' potential through creative math, inspiring messages, and innovative teaching.* San Francisco: Jossey-Bass.

Boscolo, P., Arfé, B., & Quarisa, M. (2007). Improving the quality of students' academic writing: An intervention study. *Studies in Higher Education, 32*(4), 419–438.

Boston, M. (2012). Assessing instructional quality in mathematics. *Elementary School Journal, 113*(1), 76–104.

Boston, M. D., & Wilhelm, A. G. (2017). Middle school mathematics instruction in instructionally focused urban districts. *Urban Education, 52*(7), 829–861.

Boyd, M. P., & Markarian, W. C. (2015). Dialogic teaching and dialogic stance: Moving beyond interactional form. *Research in the Teaching of English, 49*(3), 272–296.

Bradlee, B., Jr. (2018). *The forgotten: How the people of one Pennsylvania county elected Donald Trump and changed America.* New York: Little, Brown.

Bransford, J. D., Brown, A. L., & Cocking, R. R. (Eds.). (2000). *How people learn: Brain, mind, experience, and school* (Expanded ed.). Washington, DC: National Academy Press.

Bråten, I., Braasch, J. L. G., & Salmerón, L. (2017). *Reading multiple and non-traditional texts: New opportunities and new challenges.* Accessed at www.academia .edu/35213086/Reading_Multiple_and_Non-Traditional_Texts_New _Opportunities_and_New_Challenges on January 24, 2020.

Bråten, I., Ferguson, L. E., Anmarkrud, O., & Stromso, H. I. (2013). Prediction of learning and comprehension when adolescents read multiple texts: The roles of word-level processing, strategic approach, and reading motivation. *Reading and Writing, 26*(3), 321–348.

Britt, M. A., & Rouet, J. F. (2012). Learning with multiple documents: Component skills and their acquisition. In J. R. Kirby & M. J. Lawson (Eds.), *Enhancing the quality of learning: Dispositions, instruction, and learning processes* (pp. 276–314). New York: Cambridge University Press.

Brooks, D. (2018, October 15). The rich white civil war: A smarter look at America's divide. *New York Times*. Accessed at www.nytimes.com/2018/10/15/opinion /politics-race-white-tribalism.html on August 16, 2019.

Bybee, R. W., Taylor, J. A., Gardner, A., Van Scotter, P., Powell, J. C., Westbrook, A., et al. (2006). *The BSCS 5E instructional model: Origins, effectiveness, and applications.* Colorado Springs, CO: BSCS.

Caron, E. J. (2005). What leads to the fall of a great empire? Using central questions to design issues-based history units. *The Social Studies, 96*(2), 51–60.

Cawn, B. (2016). *Texts, tasks, and talk: Instruction to meet the Common Core in grades 9–12.* Bloomington, IN: Solution Tree.

Cawn, B., Ikemoto, G., & Grossman, J. (2016). *Ambitious leadership: How principals lead schools to college and career readiness.* New York: New Leaders.

Chall, J. S. (1983). *Learning to read: The great debate.* New York: McGraw-Hill.

Chinn, C. A., & Anderson, R. C. (1998). The structure of discussions that promote reasoning. *Teacher College Record, 100*(2), 315–368.

City, E. A., Elmore, R. F., Fiarman, S. E., & Teitel, L. (2009). *Instructional rounds in education: A network approach to improving teaching and learning* (6th ed.). Cambridge, MA: Harvard Education Press.

Clifton, L. (2012). Won't you celebrate with me. In K. Young & M. S. Glaser (Eds.), *The collected poems of Lucille Clifton 1965–2010.* Rochester, NY: BOA Editions.

Cobb, P., Jackson, K., Henrick, E., Smith, T. M., & the MIST Team. (2018). *Systems for instructional improvement: Creating coherence from the classroom to the district office.* Cambridge, MA: Harvard Education Press.

Cobb, P., McClain, K., de Silva Lamberg, T., & Dean, C. (2003). Situating teachers' instructional practices in the institutional setting of the school and district. *Educational Researcher, 32*(6), 13–24.

Colburn, A. (2000). An inquiry primer. *Science Scope, 23*(6), 42–44.

College Board. (n.d.). *Synthesis essay materials.* Accessed at https://apcentral .collegeboard.org/courses/ap-english-language-and-composition/classroom -resources/synthesis-essay-materials on November 14, 2019.

College Board. (2018). *AP English language and composition: Free-response questions.* Accessed at https://secure-media.collegeboard.org/ap/pdf/ap18-frq-english -language.pdf on July 26, 2019.

Collins, W., Colman, R., Haywood, J., Manning, M. R., & Mote, P. (2007). The physical science behind climate change. *Scientific American, 297*(2), 64–73.

Coombs, D., & Bellingham, D. (2015). Using text sets to foster critical inquiry. *English Journal, 105*(2), 88–95.

Daniels, H., & Zemelman, S. (2014). *Subjects matter: Exceeding standards through powerful content-area reading.* Portsmouth, NH: Heinemann.

De La Paz, S., & Felton, M. K. (2010). Reading and writing from multiple source documents in history: Effects of strategy instruction with low to average high school writers. *Contemporary Educational Psychology, 35*(3), 174–192.

Depka, E. (2017). *Raising the rigor: Effective questioning strategies and techniques for the classroom.* Bloomington, IN: Solution Tree Press.

Dever, R., & Lash, M. J. (2013). Using common planning time to foster professional learning: Researchers examine how a team of middle school teachers use common planning time to cultivate professional learning opportunities. *Middle School Journal, 45*(1), 12–17.

Douglass, F. (2014). *Narrative of the life of Frederick Douglass, an American slave.* New York: Penguin Classics.

Dweck, C. S. (2006). *Mindset: The new psychology of success.* New York: Random House.

Dyer, E. B., & Sherin, M. G. (2016). Instructional reasoning about interpretations of student thinking that supports responsive teaching in secondary mathematics. *ZDM, 48*(1–2), 69–82.

Elish-Piper, L., Wold, L. S., & Schwingendorf, K. (2014). Scaffolding high school students' reading of complex texts using linked text sets. *Journal of Adolescent and Adult Literacy, 57*(7), 565–574.

EngageNY. (n.d.). *Common Core curriculum.* Accessed at www.engageny.org/common -core-curriculum on July 25, 2019.

English, L. D. (2017). Advancing elementary and middle school STEM education. *International Journal of Science and Mathematics Education, 15*(1), 5–24.

Ericsson, K. A. (2004). Deliberate practice and the acquisition and maintenance of expert performance in medicine and related domains. *Academic Medicine, 79*(10), S70–S81.

Fisher, D., & Frey, N. (2014). Addressing CCSS anchor standard 10: Text complexity. *Language Arts, 91*(4), 236–250.

Fisher, D., Frey, N., & Hattie, J. (2016). *Visible learning for literacy, grades K–12: Implementing the practices that work best to accelerate student learning.* Thousand Oaks, CA: Corwin Press.

Fitzgerald, F. S. (1925). *The great Gatsby.* New York: Scribner.

Flake, J. (2017). *Conscience of a conservative: A rejection of destructive politics and a return to principle.* New York: Random House.

Foley, J. (2010). *The other inconvenient truth* [Video]. Accessed at www.ted.com/talks /jonathan_foley_the_other_inconvenient_truth?language=en on January 28, 2020.

Franke, M. L., Carpenter, T. P., & Battey, D. (2008). Content matters: Algebraic reasoning in teacher professional development. In J. J. Kaput, D. W. Carraher, & M. L. Blanton (Eds.), *Algebra in the early grades* (pp. 333–360). New York: Routledge.

Fullan, M., & Langworthy, M. (2013). *Towards a new end: New pedagogies for deep learning*. Seattle, WA: Collaborative Impact.

Gibbons, L. K., & Cobb, P. (2016). Content-focused coaching: Five key practices. *Elementary School Journal, 117*(2), 237–260.

Goldman, S. R., McCarthy, K. S., & Burkett, C. (2015). Interpretive inferences in literature. In E. J. O'Brien, A. E. Cook, & R. F. Lorch, Jr. (Eds.), *Inferences during reading* (pp. 386–415). Cambridge, UK: Cambridge University Press.

Goldman, S. R., Snow, C., & Vaughn, S. (2016). Common themes in teaching reading for understanding: Lessons from three projects. *Journal of Adolescent and Adult Literacy, 60*(3), 255–264.

Greenleaf, C., & Brown, W. R. (2017). An argument for learning. *Learning Professional, 38*(2), 56–60, 70.

Greenleaf, C., & Valencia, S. W. (2017). Missing in action: Learning from texts in subject-matter classrooms. In K. A. Hinchman & D. A. Appleman (Eds.), *Adolescent literacies: A handbook of practice-based research* (pp. 235–256). New York: Guilford Press.

Gregory, J. N. (2005). *The southern diaspora: How the great migrations of black and white southerners transformed America*. Chapel Hill: University of North Carolina Press.

Hartman, D. K., & Allison, J. (1996). Promoting inquiry-oriented discussions using multiple texts. In L. B. Gambrell & J. F. Almasi (Eds.), *Lively discussions: Fostering engaged reading* (pp. 106–133). Newark, DE: International Reading Association.

Hassrick, E. M., Raudenbush, S. W., & Rosen, L. (2017). *The ambitious elementary school: Its conception, design, and implications for educational equality*. Chicago: University of Chicago Press.

Hiebert, J., Gallimore, R., Garnier, H., Givvin, K., Hollingsworth, H., Jacobs, J., et al. (2003). *Teaching mathematics in seven countries: Results from the TIMSS 1999 Video Study*. Washington, DC: National Center for Education Statistics.

Hiebert, J., & Stigler, J. W. (2017). Teaching versus teachers as a lever for change: Comparing a Japanese and a U.S. perspective on improving instruction. *Educational Researcher, 46*(4), 169–176.

Hillocks, G. (2010). Teaching argument for critical thinking and writing: An introduction. *English Journal, 99*(6), 24–32.

Holmes, N. G., Day, J., Park, A. H. K., Bonn, D. A., & Roll, I. (2014). Making the failure more productive: Scaffolding the invention process to improve inquiry behaviors and outcomes in invention activities. *Instructional Science, 42*(4), 523–538.

Huff, J., Preston, C., Goldring, E., & Guthrie, J. (2018). Learning-centered leadership practices for effective high schools serving at-risk students. *Teachers College Record, 120*(9), 1–38.

Intergovernmental Panel on Climate Change. (2014). *Climate change 2013: The physical science basis*. New York: Cambridge University Press.

Intergovernmental Panel on Climate Change. (2018). *Global warming of 1.5 °C*. Accessed at https://www.ipcc.ch/sr15/ on January 28, 2020.

Iordanou, K., & Constantinou, C. P. (2015). Supporting use of evidence in argumentation through practice in argumentation and reflection in the context of SOCRATES learning environment. *Science Education, 99*(2), 282–311.

Ivey, G. (2002). Getting started: Manageable literacy practices. *Educational Leadership, 60*(3), 20–23.

Iyengar, S. & Krupenkin, M. (2018). The strengthening of partisan affect. *Advances in Political Psychology, 39*(1), 201–218.

Jackson, K., Garrison, A., Wilson, J., Gibbons, L., & Shahan, E. (2013). Exploring relationships between setting up complex tasks and opportunities to learn in concluding whole-class discussions in middle-grades mathematics instruction. *Journal for Research in Mathematics Education, 44*(4), 646–682.

Jaeger, C. C., Hasselmann, K., Leipold, G., Mangalagiu, D., & Tabara, J. D. (Eds.). (2012). *Reframing the problem of climate change: From zero sum game to win-win solutions*. New York: Earthscan.

James, K., Goldman, S. R., Ko, M., Greenleaf, C. L., & Brown, W. (2014). *Multiple-text processing in text-based scientific inquiry*. Proceedings of the 11th International Conference of the Learning Sciences, Boulder, CO.

Journell, W., Friedman, A., Thacker, E., & Fitchett, P. (2018.) Getting inquiry design just right. *Social Education, 82*(4), 202–205.

Kamil, M. L., Borman, G. D., Dole, J., Kral, C. C., Salinger, T., & Torgesen, J. (2008). *Improving adolescent literacy: Effective classroom and intervention practices: A practice guide*. Washington, DC: National Center for Education Evaluation and Regional Assistance.

Kennedy, M. M. (2016). How does professional development improve teaching? *Review of Educational Research, 86*(4), 945–980.

Kerlin, S. C., McDonald, S. P., & Kelly, G. J. (2010). Complexity of secondary scientific data sources and students' argumentative discourse. *International Journal of Science Education, 32*(9), 1207–1225.

King, P. M., & Kitchener, K. S. (2004). Reflective judgment: Theory and research on the development of epistemic assumptions through adulthood. *Educational Psychologist, 39*(1), 5–18.

Lampert, M., & Graziani, F. (2009). Instructional activities as a tool for teachers' and teacher educators' learning. *Elementary School Journal, 109*(5), 491–509.

Lee, C. D. (2007). *Culture, literacy, and learning: Taking bloom in the midst of the whirlwind*. New York: Teachers College Press.

Lee, C. D., & Spratley, A. (2010). *Reading in the disciplines: The challenges of adolescent literacy.* New York: Carnegie Corporation of New York.

Lee, H. (1960). *To kill a mockingbird.* New York: HarperCollins.

Lee, H. (2015). *Go set a watchman.* New York: Harper.

Lefstein, A. (2010). More helpful as problem than solution: Some implications of situated dialogue in classrooms. In K. Littleton & C. Howe (Eds.), *Educational dialogues: Understanding and promoting productive interaction* (pp. 170–191). London: Routledge.

Litman, C., & Greenleaf, C. (2018). Argumentation tasks in secondary English language arts, history, and science: Variations in instructional focus and inquiry space. *Reading Research Quarterly, 53*(1), 107–126.

Litman, C., Marple, S., Greenleaf, C., Charney-Sirrott, I., Bolz, M., Richardson, L., et al. (2017). Text-based argumentation with multiple sources: A descriptive study of opportunity to learn in secondary English language arts, history, and science. *Journal of the Learning Sciences, 26*(1), 79–130.

Lupo, S. M., McKenna, M. C., & Walpole, S. (2015, December). *Quad text sets: A formative approach to exploring how to scaffold adolescents in reading challenging texts.* Paper presented at the annual meeting of the Literacy Research Association, Carlsbad, CA.

Lupo, S. M., Strong, J. Z., Lewis, W., Walpole, S., & McKenna, M. C. (2018). Building background knowledge through reading: Rethinking text sets. *Journal of Adolescent and Adult Literacy, 61*(4), 433–444.

Martínez, I., Mateos, M., Martín, E., & Rijlaarsdam, G. (2015). Learning history by composing synthesis texts: Effects of an instructional programme on learning, reading and writing processes, and text quality. *Journal of Writing Research, 7*(2), 275–302.

Marzano, R. J., & Toth, M. D. (2014). *Teaching for rigor: A call for a critical instructional shift* [Monograph]. West Palm Beach, FL: Learning Sciences International.

Match Fishtank. (n.d.a). *The glass menagerie: 11th grade English.* Accessed at www .matchfishtank.org/curriculum/english-language-arts/11th-grade-english/the-glass -menagerie/ on February 3, 2020.

Match Fishtank. (n.d.b). *When I was Puerto Rican: A memoir.* Accessed at www .matchfishtank.org/curriculum/english-language-arts/7th-grade-english/when-i -was-puerto-rican-a-memoir/lesson-27/#notes on January 27, 2020.

Mathis, A. (2013). *The twelve tribes of Hattie.* New York: Vintage Books.

McCracken, H. (2014, April). How Gmail happened: The inside story of its launch ten years ago. *TIME.* Accessed at https://time.com/43263/gmail-10th-anniversary/ on November 18, 2019.

McDonald, M., Kazemi, E., & Kavanagh, S. S. (2013). Core practices and pedagogies of teacher education: A call for a common language and collective activity. *Journal of Teacher Education, 64*(5), 378–386.

McNeill, K. L., & Knight, A. M. (2013). Teachers' pedagogical content knowledge of scientific argumentation: The impact of professional development on K–12 teachers. *Science Education, 97*(6), 936–972.

Michaels, S., & O'Connor, C. (2015). Conceptualizing talk moves as tools: Professional development approaches for academically productive discussions. In L. Resnick, C. Asterhan, & S. Clarke (Eds.), *Socializing intelligence through talk and dialogue* (pp. 347–362). Washington, DC: American Educational Research Association.

Moje, E. B. (2015). Doing and teaching disciplinary literacy with adolescent learners: A social and cultural enterprise. *Harvard Educational Review, 85*(2), 254–278.

Morris, A. K., & Hiebert, J. (2011). Creating shared instructional products: An alternative approach to improving teaching. *Educational Researcher, 40*(1), 5–14.

Mourshed, M., Krawitz, M., & Dorn, E. (2017). *How to improve student educational outcomes: New insights from data analytics.* Washington DC: McKinsey & Company.

Mull, M. (1979, February 18). Bob Talbert's quotebag. *Detroit Free Press*, pp. 19C, column 5.

Munter, C., & Correnti, R. (2017). Examining relations between mathematics teachers' instructional vision and knowledge and change in practice. *American Journal of Education, 123*(2), 171–202.

Murphy, P. K., Greene, J. A., Firetto, C. M., Hendrick, B. D., Li, M., Montalbano, C., et al. (2018). Quality talk: Developing students' discourse to promote high-level comprehension. *American Educational Research Journal, 55*(5), 1113–1160.

Murphy, P. K., Wilkinson, I. A. G., Soter, A. O., Hennessey, M. N., & Alexander, J. F. (2009). Examining the effects of classroom discussion on students' comprehension of text: A meta-analysis. *Journal of Educational Psychology, 101*(3), 740–764.

National Council for the Social Studies. (2013). *College, career, and civic life (C3) framework for social studies state standards: Guidance for enhancing the rigor of K–12 civics, economics, geography, and history.* Silver Spring, MD: Author.

National Governors Association Center for Best Practices & Council of Chief State School Officers. (2010). *Common Core State Standards for English language arts and literacy in history/social studies, science, and technical subjects.* Washington, DC: Authors. Accessed at www.corestandards.org/assets/CCSSI_ELA%20Standards.pdf on January 24, 2020.

National Oceanic and Atmospheric Administration. (n.d.). *Maps and data.* Accessed at www.climate.gov/maps-data on November 14, 2019.

National Research Council. (2012). *A framework for K–12 science education: Practices, crosscutting concepts, and core ideas.* Washington, DC: The National Academies Press.

Newell, G. E., Beach, R., Smith, J., & VanDerHeide, J. (2011). Teaching and learning argumentative reading and writing: A review of research. *Reading Research Quarterly, 46*(3), 273–304.

Nist, S. L., & Simpson, M. L. (2000). College studying. In M. L. Kamil, P. B. Mosenthal, P. D. Pearson, & R. Barr (Eds.), *Handbook of Reading Research* (Vol. 3, pp. 645–666). Mahwah, NJ: Lawrence Erlbaum Associates.

Nussbaum, E. M., & Kardash, C. M. (2005). The effects of goal instructions and text on the generation of counterarguments during writing. *Journal of Educational Psychology, 97*(2), 157–169.

Ogle, D. M. (1986). K-W-L: A teaching model that develops active reading of expository text. *Reading Teacher, 39*(6), 564–570.

Papert, S. (1980). *Mindstorms: Children, computers, and powerful ideas.* New York: Basic Books.

Pearson, P. D., & Gallagher, M. C. (1983). The instruction of reading comprehension. *Contemporary Educational Psychology, 8*(3), 317–344.

Perry, W. G., Jr. (1999). *Forms of intellectual and ethical development in the college years: A scheme.* San Francisco: Jossey-Bass.

Putnam, R. D. (2000). *Bowling alone: The collapse and revival of American community.* New York: Simon & Schuster.

Pytash, K. E., Batchelor, K. E., Kist, W., & Srsen, K. (2014). Linked text sets in the English classroom. *The ALAN Review, 42*(1), 52–62.

Reisman, A. (2012). Reading like a historian: A document-based history curriculum intervention in urban high schools. *Cognition and Instruction, 30*(1), 86–112.

Rezba, R. J., Auldridge, T., & Rhea, L. (1999). *Teaching and learning the basic science skills.* Richmond, VA: Office of Elementary and Middle School Instructional Services.

Reznitskaya, A. (2012). Dialogic teaching: Rethinking language use during literature discussions. *Reading Teacher, 65*(7), 446–456.

Reznitskaya, A., Anderson, R. C., Dong, T., Li, Y., Kim, I. H., & Kim, S. Y. (2008). Learning to think well: Application of argument schema theory. In C. C. Block & S. R. Parris (Eds.), *Comprehension instruction: Research-based best practices* (pp. 196–213). New York: Guilford Press.

Robertson, A. D., Scherr, R. E., & Hammer, D. (Eds.). (2016). *Responsive teaching in science and mathematics.* New York: Routledge.

Ruiz-Primo, M. A., & Furtak, E. M. (2007). Exploring teachers' informal formative assessment practices and students' understanding in the context of scientific inquiry. *Journal of Research in Science Teaching, 44*(1), 57–84.

Ryu, S., & Sandoval, W. A. (2012). Improvements to elementary children's epistemic understanding from sustained argumentation. *Science Education, 96*(3), 488–526.

Sachs, S. (2000). American dream, no illusions; Immigrant literature now about more than fitting in. *New York Times*. Accessed at www.nytimes.com/2000/01/09/nyregion/american-dream-no-illusions-immigrant-literature-now-about-more-than-fitting-in.html on January 27, 2020.

Saye, J. W. (2017). Disciplined inquiry in social studies classrooms. In M. M. Manfra & C. M. Bolick (Eds.), *The Wiley handbook of social studies research* (pp. 336–359). Malden, MA: Wiley-Blackwell.

Schwarz, B. B. (2009). Argumentation and learning. In N. Muller Mirza & A. N. Perret-Clermont (Eds.), *Argumentation and education: Theoretical foundations and practices* (pp. 91–126). New York: Springer.

Seeley, C. L. (2017). Turning teaching upside down. *Educational Leadership*, *75*(2), 32–36.

Segev-Miller, R. (2007). Cognitive processes in discourse synthesis: The case of intertextual processing strategies. In M. Torrance, L. van Waes, & D. Galbraith (Eds.), *Writing and cognition* (pp. 231–250). Amsterdam: Elsevier.

Sewell, A., St. George, A., & Cullen, J. (2013). The distinctive features of joint participation in a community of learners. *Teaching and Teacher Education*, *31*(1), 46–55.

Shanahan, C., Bolz, M. J., Cribb, G., Goldman, S. R., Heppeler, J., & Manderino, M. (2016). Deepening what it means to read (and write) like a historian: Progressions of instruction across a school year in an eleventh grade U.S. history class. *The History Teacher*, *49*(2), 241–270.

Smarter Balanced Assessment Consortium. (2019a). *English/language arts practice test scoring guide: Grade 7 performance task*. Accessed at https://portal.smarterbalanced.org/library/en/g7-ela-practice-test-pt-scoring-guide.pdf on July 26, 2019.

Smarter Balanced Assessment Consortium. (2019b). *English/language arts practice test scoring guide: Grade 11 performance task*. Accessed at https://portal.smarterbalanced.org/library/en/grade-11-ela-practice-test-performance-task-scoring-guide.pdf on January 27, 2020.

Stadtler, M., Bromme, R., & Rouet, J.-F. (2018). Learning from multiple documents: How can we foster multiple document literacy skills in a sustainable way? In E. Manalo, Y. Uesaka, & C. A. Chinn (Eds.), *Promoting spontaneous use of learning and reasoning strategies: Theory, research, and practice for effective transfer* (pp. 46–61). New York: Routledge.

Stanford History Education Goup. (n.d.). *History lessons: Reading like a historian*. Accessed at https://sheg.stanford.edu/history-lessons on October 7, 2019.

Stein, M. K., & Lane, S. (1996). Instructional tasks and the development of student capacity to think and reason: An analysis of the relationship between teaching and learning in a reform mathematics project. *Educational Research and Evaluation*, *2*(1), 50–80.

Stiggins, R., & DuFour, R. (2009). Maximizing the power of formative assessments. *Phi Delta Kappan*, *90*(9), 640–644.

Stroupe, D., DeBarger, A. H., & Warner, N. (2017). *Making project-based learning actionable with ambitious instruction.* Accessed at www.researchgate.net/publication /312979005_Making_Project-Based_Learning_Actionable_with_Ambitious _Instruction on January 23, 2020.

Synthesis. (n.d.a). In *Dictionary.com.* Accessed at www.dictionary.com/browse /synthesis on November 14, 2019.

Synthesis. (n.d.b). In *Merriam-Webster.* Accessed at www.merriam-webster.com /dictionary/synthesis on November 14, 2019.

Talanquer, V., Bolger, M., & Tomanek, D. (2015). Exploring prospective teachers' assessment practices: Noticing and interpreting student understanding in the assessment of written work. *Journal of Research in Science Teaching, 52*(5), 585–609.

Texas Education Agency. (n.d.). *Texas essential knowledge and skills.* Accessed at https://tea.texas.gov/Academics/Curriculum_Standards/TEKS_Texas_Essential _Knowledge_and_Skills on January 13, 2020.

TNTP. (2018). *The opportunity myth: What students can show us about how school is letting them down—And how to fix it.* Accessed at https://tntp.org/assets/documents /TNTP_The-Opportunity-Myth_Web.pdf on July 10, 2019.

Tomlinson, C. A. (2003). *Fulfilling the promise of the differentiated classroom: Strategies and tools for responsive teaching.* Alexandria, VA: Association for Supervision and Curriculum Development.

Tough, P. (2012). *How children succeed: Grit, curiosity, and the hidden power of character.* Boston: Houghton Mifflin Harcourt.

Turner, E. H. (Ed.). (1993). *Jacob Lawrence: The Migration Series.* Washington, DC: Rappahannock Press.

Valencia, S. W., Wixson, K. K., & Pearson, P. D. (2014). Putting text complexity in context: Refocusing on comprehension of complex text. *Elementary School Journal, 115*(2), 270–289.

van Leeuwen, A., & Janssen, J. (2019). A systematic review of teacher guidance during collaborative learning in primary and secondary education. *Educational Research Review, 27,* 71–89.

Vance, J. D. (2016). *Hillbilly elegy: A memoir of a family and culture in crisis.* New York: HarperCollins.

Walzer, M. (1990). What does it mean to be an "American"? *Social Research, 57*(3), 591–614.

Warren, E. (2017). *This fight is our fight: The battle to save America's middle class.* New York: Metropolitan.

Washington Times. (1916, October 23). *South unable to put stop to Negro exodus.* Accessed at http://chroniclingamerica.loc.gov/lccn/sn84026749/1916-10 -23/ed-1 /seq-1/ on January 27, 2020.

Webb, N. L. (1997). *Criteria for alignment of expectations and assessments in mathematics and science education.* Research monograph no. 6. Washington, DC: Council of Chief State School Officers.

White, E. B. (1999). The ring of time. In E. B. White, *Essays of E. B. White* (pp. 178–187). New York: Perennial Classics.

Wiggins, G., & McTighe, J. (2005). *Understanding by design.* Alexandria, VA: Association for Supervision and Curriculum Development.

Wiley, J., & Voss, J. F. (1999). Constructing arguments from multiple sources: Tasks that promote understanding and not just memory for text. *Journal of Educational Psychology, 91*(2), 301–311.

Wilkerson, I. (2010). *The warmth of other suns: The epic story of America's great migration.* New York: Random House.

Wilkinson, I. A. G., & Hye Son, E. (2009). Questioning. In E. M. Anderman & L. H. Anderman (Eds.), *Psychology of classroom learning: An encyclopedia* (pp. 723–728). Detroit, MI: MacMillan Reference USA.

Williamson, G. L. (2008). A text readability continuum for postsecondary readiness. *Journal of Advanced Academics, 19*(4), 602–632.

Willingham, D. T. (2006). How knowledge helps: It speeds and strengthens reading comprehension, learning—and thinking. *American Educator, 30*(1), 30–37.

Willingham, D. T. (2018). Unlocking the science of how kids think: A new proposal for reforming teacher education. *Education Next, 18*(3), 42–49.

Wilson, M. B. (2012). *Interactive modeling: A powerful technique for teaching children.* Turners Falls, MA: Northeast Foundation for Children.

Windschitl, M., Thompson, J., & Braaten, M. (2011). Ambitious pedagogy by novice teachers: Who benefits from tool-supported collaborative inquiry into practice and why? *Teachers College Record, 113*(7), 1311–1360.

Wineburg, S. (2001). *Historical thinking and other unnatural acts: Charting the future of teaching the past.* Philadelphia: Temple University Press.

Wixson, K. K., & Valencia, S. W. (2014). CCSS-ELA suggestions and cautions for addressing text complexity. *Reading Teacher, 67*(6), 430–434.

Wolfe, M. B. W., & Goldman, S. R. (2005). Relations between adolescents' text processing and reasoning. *Cognition and Instruction, 23*(4), 467–502.

World Bank. (2012). *Turn down the heat: Why a 4°C warmer world must be avoided.* Accessed at www-wds.worldbank.org/external/default/WDSContentServer/WDSP/IB/2015/07/17/090224b0828c33e7/1_0/Rendered/PDF/Turn0down0the00orld0must0be0avoided.pdf on January 27, 2020.

Zion, M., & Mendelovici, R. (2012). Moving from structured to open inquiry: Challenges and limits. *Science Education International, 23*(4), 383–399.

INDEX

Texts, Tasks, and Talk
Brad Cawn
To fully address the Common Core State Standards, educators must pair standards-aligned instructional goals with high-quality texts. The author underscores the crucial role of text selection, close reading, task construction, classroom discussion, and collaboration in literacy instruction.
BKF645

Raising the Rigor
Eileen Depka
This user-friendly resource shares questioning strategies and techniques proven to enhance students' critical thinking skills, deepen their engagement, and better prepare them for college and careers. The author also provides a range of templates, surveys, and checklists for planning instruction, deconstructing academic standards, and increasing classroom rigor.
BKF722

Ready for Anything
Suzette Lovely
Effective teaching and learning must reflect what's happening technologically, socially, economically, and globally. In *Ready for Anything*, author Suzette Lovely introduces four touchstones that will invigorate students' curiosity and aspirations and prepare them for college, careers, and life in the 21st century.
BKF848

Real-World Learning Framework for Secondary Schools
Marge Maxwell, Rebecca Stobaugh, and Janet Lynne Tassell
Using the Create Excellence Framework, educators can help students find greater fulfillment in learning, while also meeting the guidelines of curriculum standards. Explore the framework's main components, and understand how to use the framework for classroom, school, and district pursuits.
BKF656

Solution Tree | Press

a division of
Solution Tree

Visit SolutionTree.com or call 800.733.6786 to order.

Wait! Your professional development journey doesn't have to end with the last pages of this book.

We realize improving student learning doesn't happen overnight. And your school or district shouldn't be left to puzzle out all the details of this process alone.

No matter where you are on the journey, we're committed to helping you get to the next stage.

Take advantage of everything from **custom workshops** to **keynote presentations** and **interactive web and video conferencing**. We can even help you develop an action plan tailored to fit your specific needs.

Let's get the conversation started.

Call 888.763.9045 today.

SolutionTree.com